SECOND PERSON RURAL

Noel Perrin, teacher, writer, and farmer (in that order), was city-born but country-bred. Now living in Thetford, Vermont (reputedly the last operating theocracy in America), he teaches at Dartmouth College and scours a precarious living from the flinty New England soil. His articles, reviews, and hints on animal (and human) husbandry in sources as diverse as *Country Journal* and *The New York Times Book Review* have delighted audiences nationwide. Unawed by his fame, Mr. Perrin continues to devote his time to understanding the fickle ways of nature and the feckless behavior of non-natives. He is married, a devoted father, a model author, and generally the closest thing to a rural polymath this country has produced. Mr. Perrin's *First Person Rural: Essays of a Sometime Farmer* is also published by Penguin Books.

SECOND PERSON RURAL

*More Essays of
a Sometime Farmer*

BY NOEL PERRIN

Illustrated by F. Allyn Massey

PENGUIN BOOKS

Penguin Books Ltd, Harmondsworth,
Middlesex, England
Penguin Books, 625 Madison Avenue,
New York, New York 10022, U.S.A.
Penguin Books Australia Ltd, Ringwood,
Victoria, Australia
Penguin Books Canada Limited, 2801 John Street,
Markham, Ontario, Canada L3R 1B4
Penguin Books (N.Z.) Ltd, 182–190 Wairau Road,
Auckland 10, New Zealand

First published in the United States of America by
David R. Godine, Publisher, Inc., 1980
Published in Penguin Books 1981

LIBRARY OF CONGRESS CATALOGING IN PUBLICATION DATA
Perrin, Noel.
  Second person rural.
  1. Country life—Vermont—Addresses, essays, lectures.
2. Vermont—Addresses, essays, lectures. 3. Perrin,
Noel. I. Title.
S521.5.V5P47 1981b   974.3'009'734   81-5158
ISBN 0 14 00.5920 2   AACR2

Printed in the United States of America by
R. R. Donnelley & Sons, Harrisonburg, Virginia
Set in Linotype Janson

Acknowledgments: "Country Codes," "Isn't That the Cutest Bridge!,"
"There's a Phaeton in Your Future," "The Natives Are Restless," "The
Birds, the Bees, and the Cows," "Vermont Silences," "Miniature Farm-
ing," "Cock Went A-Courting," "Life in the Fishbowl," "City Girl and
Country Mouse," "Circle of Enemies," "A Passable Farmer," and "One
Picture Is Worth Seven Cows" are reprinted by permission of *Boston*
magazine. "Planting Trees," "Cow Highway #3," "Lamb to Lamb
Chop," "One Year's Yield," "Making the Grass Grow Green," "Ten
Ton of Stun," "Falling for Apples," and "In Winter in the Woods" are
reprinted by permission of *Vermont Life*. "Best Little Woods Tool
Going," "Maple Recipes for Simpletons," "The Rural Immigration
Law," and "Pig Tales" are reprinted by permission of *Country Journal*.
"A Fool's Guide to Splitting Wood" and "The Year We *Really* Heated
with Wood" are reprinted by permission of *UpCountry*. "Garden
Animals" is reprinted by permission of *Horticulture*. All appear here
in slightly revised form.

*For Elisabeth and Amy, Manon and Kiki,
Kirk, Tracy and Jon – three sets of Vermont children.
All of them took some part in the small adventures
this book describes.*

Foreword

I HAVE ALWAYS DISTRUSTED SEQUELS. Well, not sequels per se. The Arabian Nights, which I love, consists of Scheherazade's original midnight story plus one thousand sequels. *Huckleberry Finn*, the best book Mark Twain ever wrote, is the sequel to *Tom Sawyer*. Tolkien wrote *The Lord of the Rings* as the sequel to his book about hobbits.

What I distrust are sequels that advertise themselves as such by their titles.

This phenomenon is most common in the world of children's books. An author will do one really nice book – say, the adventures of a little Ohio farm girl named Karen and her still smaller brother, Kurt. Then over the next decade fourteen more books appear, and they are successively called *Kurt and Karen Meet a Friend*, *Kurt and Karen Go to Chicago*, *Kurt and Karen's Giant Mystery Book*, and so on. Some may be good, some are sure to be worthless; all are trying to cash in on the success of the first volume. Each clutches a piece of the original title for that purpose. It's a low, contemptible practice, like the "son of" titles that used to be common in movies a generation ago, or the Roman-numeral titles that flourish now. (The only movies worth seeing, in which the final element of the title is a Roman numeral, are called things like *Henry V* and *Richard II* – and there it wasn't even Shakespeare, let alone the film producer, who put on the numeral; the Plantagenets came that way.)

In view of my contempt for Kurt-and-Karen books and *Jaws II* movies, I am a good deal surprised to find myself writing a book with just their kind of title. This book openly offers itself as a sequel to *First Person Rural*.

There are three reasons that it does. One is that I couldn't think of another title that I liked. As a matter of fact, I can rarely think of a title that I like. When the book of which this is the sequel was at the naming stage, about three years ago, I spent most of a month agonizing over what to call it. I emerged with a list of ten or fifteen notably limp possibilities. When you consider that the name at the top of the list was 'Vermont Essays,' you can imagine what the other fourteen were like. I finally sent the list in, not because I was satisfied but because I was exhausted.

Three days later my publisher phoned. (This was the man himself, David Godine.) He said calmly that every title on my list was worthless, and that therefore *he* proposed to name the book. He intended, he said, to call it *First Person Rural*.

I know a piece of serendipity when I hear it. Though my usual tendency is to resist editorial suggestions from publishers, particularly when they sound so much like editorial commands, I accepted David's title with actual cries of joy. I still like it so much that it makes every kind of sense to me to use it again, suitably adapted.

My second excuse is that there is no danger of this thing turning into a Kurt-and-Karen. It can't. Even if I get tempted, the laws of English grammar will prevent me. A series of three is the absolute maximum they will permit. This is a reassuring thought.

The third reason is the one that will make it impossible for me ever to feel really high-minded about the K.-and-K. sort of title again. I am afraid I do want to cash in on the (modest) success of the first book. If people who bought that also want to buy this, I find I want to give them a chance.

That being the case, I need in fairness to add a warning. There is some difference between the two books. The first one, though it contained rural essays of many kinds, had a fairly heavy emphasis on how to do things. There were articles on how to buy a truck, how to pick a chainsaw, how to make butter, how to cut fence posts, and so on.

This book is considerably less practical. There are still essays of the homeliest kind: how to use a peavey, what to do with maple syrup (besides pouring it on waffles), how to replace your Rototiller with a garden animal. But the main thrust of the book is on intangibles. A lot of the essays discuss differences between the city and the country, and especially differences in psychology.

So people with country places should be warned: This book will have relatively little down-to-earth advice for you. I like to think you may find it handy in dealing with your neighbors, but you won't learn from it whether to borrow a disk harrow, or rent a brush hog, or buy twenty goats, if you're setting out to restore an old field. Maybe that will come in *Third Person Rural*. At least, if it's ever going to, it will.

NOEL PERRIN
January, 1980

Contents

Contents

Second Person Rural

More Essays of a Sometime Farmer

Country Codes

ROBERT FROST ONCE WROTE a poem about a 'town-bred' farmer who was getting his hay in with the help of two hired men, both locals. As they're working, the sky clouds over, and it begins to look like rain. The farmer instructs the two hired men to start making the haycocks especially carefully, so that they'll shed water. About half an hour later (it still isn't raining), one of them abruptly shoves his pitchfork in the ground and walks off. He has quit.

The farmer is utterly baffled. The hired man who stays explains to him that what he said was a major insult.

> *'He thought you meant to find fault with his work.*
> *That's what the average farmer would have meant.'*

This hired man goes on to say that he would have quit, too – if the order had been issued by a regular farmer. But seeing as it was a city fellow, he made allowances.

> *'I know you don't understand our ways.*
> *You were just talking what was in your mind,*
> *What was in all our minds, and you weren't hinting.'*

Frost called that poem 'The Code.' He published it in 1914.

Sixty-four years later, the country code is still going strong, and it is still making trouble for town-bred people who live in rural areas. Only I think the code is even more complicated than

Frost had room to describe in his poem. In fact, there isn't just one country code, there are at least three. What they all have in common is that instead of saying things out plainly, the way you do in the city, you approach them indirectly. You hint.

I am going to call these three the Power Code, the Non-Reciprocity Code, and the Stoic's Code. These are not their recognized names; they don't *have* recognized names. Part of the code is that you never speak of the code, and I am showing my own town-bredness in writing this exposition. (As Frost showed his in writing the poem. He was a city kid in San Francisco before he was a farmer in New Hampshire.)

In Frost's poem, it was the Power Code that the townie violated. Under the rules of the Power Code, you *never* give peremptory orders, and you ordinarily don't even make demands. You make requests. What the code says is that everybody is to be treated as an equal, even when financially or educationally, or whatever, they're not. Treat them as either inferiors or superiors, and you can expect trouble.

Just recently, for example, a young city doctor moved to our town, and began violating the Power Code right and left. Take the way he treated the boss of the town road crew. The house the doctor was renting has a gravel driveway that tends to wash out after storms. It washed out maybe a month after he had moved in. He is said to have called the road commissioner and given him a brisk order. 'I want a culvert installed, and I want it done by this weekend.'

Now in the city that would be a quite sensible approach. You're calling some faceless bureaucrat, and you use standard negotiating technique. You make an outrageous demand; you throw your weight around, if you have any; and you figure on getting part of what you ask for. You're not surprised when the bureaucrat screams, *'This week!* Listen, we got a hunnert and sixty-two jobs aheada you right now. If you're lucky, we'll get to you in October.' You scream back and threaten to call the mayor's office. Then you finally compromise on August.

But it doesn't work that way in the country. The code doesn't encourage throwing your weight around. Our road commissioner had been given an order, and he instantly rejected it. ' 'Tain't the town's job to look after folks' driveways. If you want a culvert, you can buy one down to White River Junction.'

I happened to hear what the road commissioner told some friends later. The doctor had actually called at a good time. The town had several used culverts lying around – road culverts they had replaced, which were still good enough to go at the end of a driveway. 'If he'd asked decent, we'd have been glad to put one in for him, some day when work was slack.' If he'd used the code, that is.

That's nothing, though, compared with the way the young doctor handled one of our retired farmers. When the doctor decided to live in our town – it meant a fifteen-mile drive to the hospital where he worked – it was because he had gotten interested in country things. He wanted to have a garden, burn wood, learn how to scythe a patch of grass, all those things. During his first spring and summer in town, he probably asked the old farmer a hundred questions. He got free lessons in scything. He consulted on fencing problems. Learned how thick to plant peas.

Then one day the farmer asked *him* a question. 'I understand you know suthin' about arthritis,' the farmer said. 'Well, my wife's is actin' up.' And he went on to ask a question about medication.

The young doctor's answer was quick and smooth. 'I'll be glad to see her in office hours,' he said.

Again, normal city practice. You've got to protect yourself against all the people at cocktail parties who want free medical advice. Furthermore, you probably really should examine a patient before you do any prescribing. All the same, what he was saying loud and clear in the country code was, 'My time is worth more than yours; I am more important than you are. So I can ask you free questions, but you must pay for any you ask me.' Not very polite. What he should have done was put down the scythe and say, 'Let's go have a look at her.'

Actually, if he had done that, he probably would have muffed it anyway. Because then he would have come up against the Non-Reciprocity Code, and he didn't understand that, either. The Non-Reciprocity Code says that you never take any favors for granted (or call in your debts, as city politicians say). Instead, you always pretend that each favor done you is a brand-new one. In the case of the young doctor, suppose he *had* stopped his free scythe lesson and gone to examine the farmer's wife. When he was ready to leave, the farmer would have said to him, 'What do I owe you?' And then one of two things would have happened. Old habits would have asserted themselves, and he would have said smoothly, 'That will be twenty-five dollars, please.' Or else, a little cross with the farmer for not recognizing his generous motive (does the old fool think I make *house calls?*), he would have said that it was free, in a sort of huffy, look-what-a-favor-I'm-doing-you voice.

Both answers would have been wrong. The correct response would be to act as if the farmer was doing *you* a favor in letting you not charge. Something like, 'Come on, if you can teach me to scythe, and how to plant peas, I guess there's no harm in my taking a look at your wife.'

One of the funniest instances in which you see the Non-Reciprocity Code operating is after people get their trucks stuck, which during mud season in Vermont is constantly. You're driving along in your pickup, and there's your neighbor with two wheels in the ditch, unable to budge. You stop, get out your logging chain, hook on, and pull him out. 'How much will that be?' he asks, as if his cousin Donald hadn't just pulled you out the week before. In a way it's a ritual question. He would be surprised out of his mind if you thought a minute and said, 'Oh, I guess five dollars would be about right.'

But it's not entirely ritual. He would be surprised. But he would hand over the five dollars. The point of the question is to establish that you don't *have* to pull him out just because he's a friend and will someday pull you out. It's treated as an act of free will, a part of New England independence.

The third code, the Stoic's Code, is sometimes confused with machismo, but really has no connection with it. Country people of both sexes practice it with equal fervency. Basically, it consists of seeing who can go without complaining longest.

I first became aware of the Stoic's Code when I was helping two people put hay bales into a barn loft about fifteen years ago. It was a hot day in late June, with the humidity running at least ninety percent. I function badly in hot weather. Within ten minutes I was pouring sweat – as were my coworkers. The difference was that I kept bitching about it. Finally, after three-quarters of an hour, I flopped down and announced I'd have to cool off before I touched another bale.

To me this just seemed common sense. We had no special deadline to meet in loading that hay. What I really thought was that all three of us should go take a dip in the river.

But the Stoic's Code doesn't stress common sense. It stresses endurance. Maybe that's because to survive at all as a farmer in New England you need endurance. In any case, the other two flicked me one quick scornful look and kept on working. One of them has never really respected me again to this day. The other, like the second hired man in Frost's poem, made allowances for my background and forgave me. We have since become fast friends. I have never dared to ask, but I think he thinks I have made real progress in learning to shut my mouth and keep working.

I could never be a stoic on the true native level, though. Consider the story of Hayden Clark and Rodney Palmer, as Rodney tells it. A good many years ago, before there were any paved roads in town, Hayden ran a garage. (Rodney runs it now.) He also sold cordwood.

One day when there wasn't much doing at the garage, Hayden was sawing cordwood just across the road, where he could keep an eye on the gas pumps. If you saw with a circular saw, and do it right, it takes three men. One person lifts up the logs, one does the actual cutting, and one throws the cut pieces into a pile. The three jobs are called putting on, sawing, and taking off. In all three you are doing dangerous work at very high speed.

On this day a man named Charlie Raynes was putting on, Hayden was sawing, and young Rodney was taking off. Hayden kept the wood coming so fast that Rodney was always a beat behind. He never paused a second to let Rodney catch up, and this torture went on for nearly an hour. No one spoke. (Not that you could hear over a buzz saw, anyway.)

Then finally a customer pulled in for gas. Hayden left the other two sawing, and went over to pump it. Charlie continued to put on, and Rodney sawed in Hayden's place.

Rather than interrupt their rhythm when he came back, Hayden began to take off. Rodney and Charlie exchanged a quick glance, and began putting the wood to Hayden so fast that *he* was off balance the whole time, and not infrequently in some danger of getting an arm cut off. At this speed and in this way they finished the entire pile. It was Rodney's revenge, and as he told me about it, his eyes gleamed.

It was only a year or two ago that Rodney told me the story. In the very act of telling it, he included me as one who knew the code. But I instantly betrayed it. My city background is too strong. I'm too verbal, too used to crowing over triumphs.

'After you were done sawing, Hayden never said anything about it?' I asked.

'Oh, *no*,' Rodney answered, looking really shocked. 'Any more than I'd have said anything to him.'

So, next time you're in a country store and you get a sense that the locals are avoiding you as if you had the worst case of B.O. in the county, you can be pretty sure of the reason. You've probably just said some dreadful thing in code.

Isn't That the Cutest Bridge!

THERE ARE 108 COVERED BRIDGES left in Vermont. I am lucky enough to live fifty yards from one of them – close enough so that we can see it out the living-room windows.

It's not one of the great showpiece bridges of the state, but it's handsome. Someone with a good eye designed it, about a hundred years ago. From our house you see the west portal, painted a classic barn red, and you see one of the long boarded sides. The sides are unpainted, and they long ago turned the classic silvery gray of weathered barn boards.

Stroll inside, and the view is even better. Two great curved wooden beams carry the bridge in a single span over the Pompanoosuc River, and those beams have something of the solemnity of the piers in a Gothic cathedral. They are so massive and so obviously handmade. One marvels at the skill of the men who put them up.

Not that the view in there is *entirely* solemn. Old notices for long-vanished patent medicines are still glued to the beams. You can spot ancient hearts and initials carved high up.

Perhaps the best view of all is on a winter evening when it's snowing. The last village streetlight is at the far end of the bridge from our house. In its light you can see the snowflakes drifting down past the portals. There is something hushed and almost holy about such a moment.

It's a kind of miracle that the old bridge is still there. Once

© ALLYN MASSEY 1980

our town had five covered bridges – in fact, it had five covered
bridges as recently as 1950. Then the Corps of Engineers built
a flood-control dam downstream. (It's one of several dozen they
have on the various tributaries of the Connecticut River – all of
them designed to enable developers to build further out on the
floodplain around Hartford, Connecticut, and Springfield, Massachusetts.) Two covered bridges were in the way of the dam,
and the Engineers pulled them down. A third perished through
local poverty and neglect.

A couple of years after I moved to town, our bridge almost
became the fourth to go. It was beginning to sag. Instead of
spending town money to repair it, the selectmen wanted to get
some state aid and put up a modern concrete highway bridge.
A nice wide one. In this plan they were supported, even pushed,
by the one important businessman in town, and by all the local
loggers.

In the primitive democracy of a small Vermont town, however, such things have to be voted on in town meeting. A good
many natives *liked* the old bridge, and of course all us new-
comers were hysterically eager to keep it. There were plenty of
concrete bridges back where we came from. Ugly as sin, most
of them. The first time I ever spoke in town meeting was in
defense of the old bridge. And aided by the local patriarch
(he'd carved *his* initials about 1906) and by testimony from a
couple of covered-bridge clubs, we defenders scored a great
victory. The town voted overwhelmingly to repair the covered
bridge.

That decision has given pleasure to a lot of people. Sometimes
in the summer a whole caravan of covered-bridge lovers will
pull in from Massachusetts and prowl around taking pictures.
At least twice a painter has set up an easel in my front meadow,
and sat there on a little stool painting The Old Covered Bridge.
(Once, going out to mow hay, I saw an artist on her stool gazing so intently at the bridge that she utterly failed to notice
the six cows standing just behind her, gazing intently at her.
Cows can move as quietly as deer when they want to.)

For a few years the decision gave me nothing but pleasure, too. I suppose the first time a tiny doubt entered my mind was on one of those hushed winter evenings. It was a wet snow that was falling through the lamplight, and instead of standing there gazing reverently, I was driving home from work.

Since rivers have the habit of being at the bottom of valleys, the road comes downhill to each end of the bridge. And since the bridge was built for horse traffic (how else would you have time to read the patent medicine signs?), it is not wide enough for two cars easily to pass.

Coming down the east hill, a little too fast, I glanced as usual to see if there was a car coming down the west hill. There was. I put on my brakes ... and kept coming as fast as before. He did the same, both of us sliding noiseless in the snow.

We didn't actually hit. Once we both slid onto the bridge, where the roadway was bare, we stopped – at least eight or ten feet from a head-on collision. But I did reflect, as I backed out, that this wouldn't have happened if the selectmen had won.

A year or two later, I had to be away from Vermont for nine months, and I rented the house to a young doctor who was just getting out of the navy. He had been stationed in Charleston, South Carolina. His wife wrote and asked if they could ship their furniture on ahead. (I was divorced then, and the house had room after empty room.) I said sure.

About a week before they were due to arrive and I to leave, I was up cutting firewood on a mountain. (You always cut it a year in advance.) Suddenly I looked up to see the town constable puffing up the hill. 'Noel,' he said, 'there's a moving van down by the covered bridge. Wants to get to your house. Guess he could use a little help.'

Our bridge is not only narrow, it's relatively low. Back in horse days, the tallest vehicles it had to accommodate were hay wagons, and a load of loose hay is seldom more than ten feet high. So the bridge has eleven-foot clearance. Local movers know that, and use their smaller trucks.

But what was waiting on the far side of the bridge when I

reluctantly went down was a monster van from South Carolina –
a truck obscenely big. The driver was a red-haired South Caro-
linian who clearly regarded the covered bridge and the winding
back roads of Vermont as two more proofs of Yankee deceit
and incompetence. And he really did have problems. The truck
was so big that he not only had my navy doctor's furniture
aboard, but the total possessions of three other families. *They*
all lived in civilized places like Providence and Newton Lower
Falls.

We were less than a hundred yards from my house, but also
quite a lot downhill from it. The navy doctor's furniture ran
to heavy oak tables and large Victorian bureaus – many tables
and many bureaus. We never even considered trying to carry
it by hand through the bridge, or off-loading onto a pickup. The
only thing was to go around by road. We couldn't even take
the twelve-mile circuit through Union Village, because that's
where the other covered bridge in town is. No, Billy-Bob and
I had to drive clear back to Route 5, go ten miles south, and
then up a whole different set of roads. Twenty-five miles in all.
My chief diversion en route was listening to him pop his gum.
What with his having to stop and get gas on the way (it takes
a while to pump 142 gallons), it was dusk when we finally
pulled in my driveway.

'Cain't unload now,' Billy-Bob said mournfully. 'We need
daylight to see inside thet truck.' Then he gave me a mildly
hopeful look. 'What you got for motels around heah? Is there
a Holiday Inn?'

The nearest Holiday Inn is many miles away, a fact that on
every other night of my life I have considered a virtue. I wound
up giving Billy-Bob dinner, letting him use the phone to call his
dispatcher and his wife, putting him up for the night. And I
reflected that this wouldn't have happened if the selectmen had
won.

Just these past few months I've been doing some logging. Cut
a bunch of big basswoods behind the house. The mill I want
to take them to is on my side of the bridge – two miles away.

I thought of that before I started cutting. But I didn't think enough about how I would get them there. The two men I know with logging trucks both live on the far side. A logging truck with boom will not go through an eleven-foot bridge. Neither man is crazy to take a twenty-five-mile drive to pick up my few logs, carry them two miles to the sawmill, and then drive twenty-five miles home. I can't help reflecting that . . .

It's a beautiful bridge, and I still love it. But when a native friend looks at it thoughtfully, as one did in my presence not long ago, and muses out loud, 'It wouldn't take more'n about one match on that dry wood,' I do understand what he's talking about.

Planting Trees

A FRIEND OF MINE who grew up on the Western prairies
bought a place in Vermont a few years ago. There is one good
hayfield left from the days when it was a farm, and maybe two
clear acres around the house. All the rest is trees.

About a week after he bought the place, Matt and I took a
walk along his boundaries. Naturally we were mostly in the
woods. We climbed up a hillside covered with young oaks. We
followed old wire along the edge of an ex-field now thick with
gray birch and poplars. From there we emerged into a cathedral
stand of spruce – sixty-footers with great sweeping boughs. Matt
looked at them in real awe. 'My word!' he said. 'Someone must
have worked awfully hard to plant all these trees!'

It took him a while to accept the idea that every single tree
he owned (except the maples around the house and a few fruit
trees) had been planted by another tree . . . and that what his
predecessors on the farm had worked hard at was getting rid of
trees. If you've grown up in a sea of grass, with maybe two
man-planted willows on a 160-acre farm, I can see that this
would be a novel idea.

I have since come to suspect that most people who work for
the U.S. Department of Agriculture also grew up on the Great
Plains. At any rate, they clearly believe that if there are going
to be enough trees in Vermont, we had all better be out there
planting them. In fact, they'll pay us to do it. Back when I was

a newcomer and didn't know any better, they paid me for three years running.

That was in the early sixties. I had just had my farm for a year or two, and was eager to do some farming. I didn't own the equipment you need to plant and harvest crops (and would have been scared to try, anyway); and I was too inexperienced even to dream of keeping cattle. So when I found that the government had an official program for planting trees and joining it automatically defined you as a farmer, I practically fell over myself on the way to the county office.

The way the program worked was this. First you signed up. Then the county forester came and checked out your land. Then, if he approved, you could order your trees, either pines or spruces. You ordered in multiples of a thousand, and the Department of Agriculture agreed to pay you thirty-four dollars for each thousand that you planted. Since a thousand seedlings cost only fourteen dollars, you wound up with a profit of two cents per tree. No fortune, I admit, but it *was* money earned by working your place.

As for the actual planting, the only equipment you needed was a bucket to hold the seedlings and a mattock to dig the holes. No skill or intelligence required. The one thing the government insisted was that you plant the trees in land that was completely open. That is, pasture, or hayfield, or cropland.

I had plenty of such land. The best of it was used by a neighboring farmer, but there were several bits and pieces just going to waste. A little hayfield right behind the house, for example. A small sloping pasture below the orchard. And so on. Enough to keep me planting for years.

That first year – it was 1964 – I ordered a thousand red pines. The next year I figured I might do two thousand. They arrived on the fifth of May, about a week after the last traces of frost had gone out of the ground, and I put in three long, hard days planting them. (Midafternoon on the second day I decided just to do a thousand the next year, after all.) Two-thirds went to fill in the slope in front of the orchard, and with the other third

I began on the field behind the house. The little pine seedlings looked cute, there in the grass.

That summer Vermont had a devastating drought, and about seven hundred of my cute little trees died. The ones behind the house did better than the ones in front of the orchard, because by putting three garden hoses together, I was able laboriously to water a good many of them. But even so, most of them turned brown and expired.

We farmers are a stubborn lot. The next year, ordering another thousand, I systematically replaced every dead tree. The three hundred extras I used to extend the planting behind the house.

Vermont weather is equally stubborn. In 1965 the drought was even worse. At least nine hundred of the new trees died. This included nearly all the new ones behind the house, since my spring was not yielding enough water to do laundry, let alone water trees. I am not complaining. Most springs in town were dry.

If Vermont farmers quit when things went badly, there wouldn't be any Vermont farmers. In 1966 I ordered still another thousand. This time, in consultation with the county forester, I made it half red pine and half spruce, hoping one kind or the other would survive.

The drought ended that year. Nearly all of both kinds survived – say, 990 healthy seedlings. The little spruces looked even cuter than the little pines, there among the buttercups and grasses.

Good growing weather followed for the next eight years. My little trees grew and thrived. The pines got to be ten feet tall. The spruces had solid phalanxes of branches covering an area five feet in diameter. The buttercups were gone. So was my sense of satisfaction. In fact, the trees were now making me nervous. During those eight years I had learned a fair amount about farming – such as how to keep cattle, build fences, take care of an orchard. (The first thing is to keep it from being shaded – for example, by growing ranks of red pines.) I had come to realize that what I wanted behind the house was not a forest but my hayfield.

It's not easy, though, to decide to cut down thriving young trees, especially if you've planted them yourself, and most especially if you've planted them three times. The first year in my new frame of mind I did no more than cut one of the spruces, trim it down a little, and use it for a Christmas tree. The next year I managed to give fourteen friends rather hefty Christmas trees – which, with our own, got rid of fifteen. Too slow! The following summer I just boldly cut down whole ranks of pines and spruces mixed, and let them lie. I suppose I got two hundred. That saves the best part of the field behind our house – and incidentally our view. What I'm going to do about the orchard I still don't know. Some of those red pines are now eighteen feet tall, and growing, growing, growing ...

Spring is tree-planting time in Vermont. But except on steep hillsides and in barren sandy places, no farmer in his right mind is going to plant any. (I do not, of course, count fruit trees, or a few maples around the house.)

What farmers do in the spring is to mow for dear life, hoping to remove baby trees from the fields as fast as other trees plant them there, hoping to cope with the permanent population explosion of oak, birch, and pine for one more year.

Cow Highway #3

HOW DO YOU MOVE a bunch of cattle from one pasture to another some distance away? Well, some people walk backwards toward the new pasture, calling 'Coom, Bos' and temptingly holding out a bucket of grain. The cows come trailing after. Others prefer to drive the herd from behind. They gather the whole family, put a guard out on each side, and themselves walk in back, holding a pitchfork and shouting 'Git along!'

Still others seek nonhuman assistance. They load two cows at a time in a pickup and drive them to the new pasture as you might drive the kids to school. They play cowboy (or, in the West, possibly *are* cowboys) and herd them on horseback. Or, for super-stubborn cattle, they use a tractor. I still treasure the memory of Ed Paige's two-year-old bull going down the road a few years ago. Ed was driving the tractor. Behind the tractor was a heavy wooden cart. Behind the cart, and tied to it with a rope, was the bull. He had all four legs as stiff as he could make them; they were set at about a thirty-degree angle forward. The tractor groaned along in low gear, and the bull came sliding after, motionless as a statue. When Ed turned off the paved road onto his hay lane, the bull's four hooves began making furrows three inches deep. You could have plowed your garden with that bull.

Then there is one more way. You can build a cow highway, and let the cows move themselves.

19

There are two new cow highways in Thetford this year. Ed Paige's twenty-two-year-old son, Ellis, built one of them, and my old friend Floyd Dexter built the other. Both were constructed with barbwire and homemade fence posts.

Ellis's highway is 230 yards long and ten feet wide. Its function is to let his six Angus and part-Angus beef cattle walk from their regular pasture along the edge of a hayfield, around a corner, past a small cornfield, and into Warren DeMont's backyard. The question immediately arises, Why does he want them in Warren's backyard? The answer is that it's a backyard scaled to country proportions: it contains two and a half acres of first-class grazing. For his part, Warren is delighted to see them come. They not only mow the yard for free, they are eliminating the burdocks by the simple process of eating them.

If there were a brook running through Warren's, or even a wet spot on the place, there would probably be no highway. It would then make sense for Ellis just to take a couple of cows over and park them for the summer. But there is neither, and cows are big drinkers. Ellis can't possibly be running them back and forth in his truck every time they get thirsty. He'd never finish building his house. Especially since he is building it from so close to scratch. He started by buying a small sawmill. Then he cut trees, and sawed out the lumber. Now he's framing the house up. Since he also has a regular job, and in addition is the chief of the Thetford Volunteer Fire Department, the cows simply cannot expect his full-time attendance.

Anyone who drives through town and uses his eyes can see Ellis's highway, and the cow traffic moving back and forth. But Floyd's highway is secret. When his three milk cows emerge at the far end, it seems a kind of magic.

To visualize it, you must first see the village of Thetford Center in your mind's eye. As you drive into it on Vermont State Highway 113, you are conscious of a few houses on each side of the road. Floyd's is the last one on the right before you reach the center of town. Then you pass a small group of brick buildings that *are* the center of town. They're on the right, too.

First is a sort of little mausoleum for Thetford's one Revolutionary War hero. Then the town hall, then the church. Both of these are rosy brick from the 1830s. Then come the store and the Betts place, which are clapboard, and then Dr. Hopkins's house, also old brick. Behind the church you can see the cemetery, with open fields at both ends. Behind that the trees begin, climbing up the side of Meeting House Hill.

You didn't know it, but all this time you were driving parallel to Floyd's cow highway. It starts where the back of his pasture touches the woods. It runs along just inside the trees – past the mausoleum, the town hall, the church, the store, Mrs. Betts's, and Dr. Hopkins's. After a quarter-of-a-mile run, it emerges in a field belonging to Enoch Hill. It has crossed property belonging to four different people. While you were idling along, admiring the town house and the church, maybe getting a little gas at the store, little did you dream that a brisk traffic in Guernseys was going past you in both directions. Since Floyd lives right in the village, his home pasture is maybe half an acre – nothing to three hungry cows. Their practice is to trot down their highway right after morning milking and eat clover in Enoch's field all morning. Along about one o'clock they come home for a drink. They may stay home for the afternoon and chew cud, or they may hurry back to Enoch's for more clover. Around five it's time to hit the road again – back home for a light supper of grain and evening milking. Then it's usually back to Enoch's for the night.

In the city, it's people who commute. In the country, it's cows.

Lamb to Lamb Chop

FALL IS HARVEST TIME. You pick your last apples, you gather the butternuts, you dig the carrots and potatoes – you harvest every crop that remains. If you've been raising any animals for meat, you also harvest them.

This past fall I harvested four lambs. It was a new experience. No animal has been butchered on this farm in the fifteen years I've owned it. I've sent many pigs and a few beef cattle off to *be* butchered, but I've never held the knife in my own hands before. I'm not sure I'll do it again any time soon. But I am glad to have tried it once. I'm even gladder that I had a friend who did nearly all the hard parts.

Our lambs died on October 8th. This part of Vermont had had its first killing frost a few days earlier. The grass was done growing, and the sheep pasture was down to the roots. About nine o'clock on Saturday morning, my friend George deNagy arrived with his .22 single-shot rifle and his array of knives. There is a big maple next to the sheep pasture, which we picked for the scene of the butchering. We slung a rope over a branch about ten feet up, and tied an iron hook on one end. Then we went into the pasture. George took careful aim just behind the ear of one of the lambs, and shot. It was a perfect shot. The lamb died instantly, and within a few seconds we had his carotid artery cut; the still-beating heart pumped all his blood out onto the grass. The other three lambs continued placidly to graze.

All this time there was a tense silence from the house. Inside were three disapproving children: my thirteen-year-old daughter, Amy, and my stepdaughters, Manon and Kiki, who are eleven and nine. All three of them are fond of lamb chops, but they prefer to think of these objects as materializing in pre-wrapped supermarket packages, rather than connecting them with any actual living creature. So do I, for that matter. It's one reason I wanted to slaughter on the place this year. If we both raise sheep and eat mutton, at some point we need to make the connection.

By eleven o'clock we had a small crowd in the yard. George was on his third lamb. Two were skinned, and I had hung them in the barn basement, ready to be cut up the next day. One was suspended from the maple tree, and one was still in the pasture, baaing a little. Not, so far as I could tell, because he had perceived the death of the other three, but merely because he had perceived their absence. Sheep hate to be alone.

A friend of both George's and mine, a young doctor named Andy Rowles, was trying his hand at skinning the third lamb. Andy graduated from medical school five years ago, and has been leading a sort of Dagwood-sandwich life since then. First he does a year of medical training, then he spends a year living pioneer style on his Vermont hillside, then back to training, and so on. A full-time pioneer named Robert Dunn and his girl, Ceci, were watching.

But that still wasn't the whole crowd. Just as Andy started his turn on the third lamb, the kitchen door opened, and three children came out to watch.

I wasn't sure I was glad they had come. The view consisted of a half-skinned and headless lamb, with Andy deftly at work on it; and, close by, a wheelbarrow containing the three heads, and all the other debris. Furthermore, there really and truly is a smell of death, and it was present. I was afraid they might turn and run sobbing back to the house.

They didn't. They stayed throughout the dressing (which is really undressing) of the third lamb. They asked questions about everything in the wheelbarrow. Sometimes they were horrified, but mostly they were fascinated.

When it came time to shoot the fourth lamb, the two younger girls quietly drifted off toward the river, but Amy chose to stay and watch. She did cry afterwards, and she told me that she intended to eat none of the meat of these lambs, ever, but she stayed and watched. I even think she is a little more in control of her own feelings about death than she was before.

On Sunday we cut, wrapped, and froze our lambs. All except the scraps, coming to something like three and a half pounds per lamb, which I took on Monday to a local grocery store to be ground into lambburger. (It costs ten cents a pound, and they do it at the end of the day, just before they wash the grinder. It's a lot easier than putting all that meat through the hand grinder at home.)

Monday night we had lambburgers for dinner. At this point something really interesting happened. As we sat down, Manon, the eleven-year-old, looked suspiciously at her plate, and said, 'What kind of meat is this, Mommy?'

'Ground lamb, dear. You'll like it.'

'Is it from . . .'

'No, dear, it's from Dan and Whit's.'

All three girls promptly attacked their meat, and all three ate every bite. From a taste point of view, this is no great wonder. People who have had so-called lamb patties in restaurants have no idea how good fresh lambburger is. It tastes just like lamb chops – and, in fact, we don't call it lambburger any more; we call it ground lamb chop.

But the interesting thing is what went on in their minds. On Saturday they had watched a lamb being skinned. They knew that on Sunday I had spent most of the day with George cutting lambs up. On Monday we had lamb for dinner. They readily accepted their mother's statement that the lamb was from the store. (Not quite a lie, either, because it *was* at Dan and Whit's that the meat was ground.)

Girls of nine, eleven, and thirteen can be much harder than

that to convince, can be impossible to convince. It seems to me that they had a will to be reassured, and that on some level they knew perfectly well what they were eating. Even as people at McDonald's know perfectly well that, disguise it as you will with a yellow plastic box, a bun, pickles, special sauce, and God knows what else, it is finally a fellow living creature that one goes there to consume.

Only Amy, Manon, and Kiki had their knowledge on a level much nearer consciousness than people mostly do at McDonald's. And I would claim that they are that much nearer to accepting full humanity.

One Year's Yield

THE COMMON FATE of part-time farmers is to be sneered at. Real farmers regard us with the amused tolerance a racing driver might feel for a small child pedaling down the sidewalk, making motor noises in his throat. They're feeding the nation; we're not even feeding our families with our tiny crops.

Visitors from the city, on the other hand, see us as people on whom the country is wasted. All those golden afternoons! We *could* be fishing. We could be rambling over the hills with binoculars and bird book, or lying under an apple tree reading, or getting a tan down on the dock. Instead we're out doing our miniature version of farm work. What we get is dirty.

Even the people who sell us equipment smile a little. We buy 'junior' tractors. The two-by-six evaporator that we use to make maple syrup is called the Pleasure Model. I blush furiously every time I reflect that I do my boiling with a 'Pleasure Model.'

Are we really just playing? Or does part-time farming accomplish something? Last year I decided to keep close records and find out. At the end of the year I would know exactly how many hours I had put in, and what I had to show for them (besides pleasure). Such as, had I made any money? Would a good microscope reveal any effect on the gross national product? The tally is now complete, and I'm ready to share it. What follows is a report on what one part-time Vermont farm produced in 1977.

FIREWOOD. During the year I spent 232 hours cutting trees down, splitting logs, loading firewood in trucks, unloading it again, sharpening chainsaws, and so forth. All this labor yielded 17¾ cords of firewood – 10 for ourselves and 7¾ that I sold. After expenses, I had a cash profit of $260. That comes to $1.12 an hour, less than half the minimum wage.

That's a poor beginning. But not a hopeless one. Because it's obviously fair to count money not spent as well as cash received. Most of the wood we kept was for heating our big old farmhouse. The last year it was heated entirely with oil (about ten years ago), it took 1,750 gallons. This past winter the furnace used 338 gallons, though it was a colder winter. So I saved at least 1,400 gallons of oil. At 52¢ a gallon, that comes to $728. Now my hourly wage rises to $4.22, which is considerably better.

As for gross national product, the whole 17¾ cords is equal to just about 3,000 gallons of fuel oil. Deduct the 26 gallons of gas and oil my chainsaw used during the year, and about 15 gallons of gas the truck used in making wood deliveries, and there is 2,959 gallons of oil the country didn't have to import. (Or 14 tons of coal no one had to mine.)

Finally, I claim one intangible benefit. Every single tree that I cut for firewood I cut for other reasons as well. Mostly I was taking big bad red maples out of virtuous young stands of sugar maple, oak, and ash. Red maples, once they get a foot or so in diameter, begin to rot in the middle about as fast as they add new growth on the perimeter – and they meanwhile keep extending their top branches and stealing all the light. As many as five hundred better trees have now inherited that light. And because when you take a tree down for firewood, you can use the branches down to stuff two inches or even an inch and a half in diameter, there is no mess left in the woods. On the contrary, the six acres where I cut are looking particularly neat and clean.

OTHER WOOD PRODUCTS. I spent another 174 hours fiddling around with trees. My cash return was 90¢ for two hemlock fence posts that I sold. But there were all sorts of noncash returns. For example, I traded 30 fence posts for the right to graze our horse in a neighbor's field. (The fence posts went to repair her fence.) I still possess 81 fence posts made during the year. I made enough boards by cutting hemlock logs in half with my chainsaw to put siding on the new woodshed, thus saving $26.40 in boards I didn't have to buy. And I cut no hemlock especially to make those boards. They were butt logs, too big to make fence posts. (For that matter, I cut no hemlocks especially to make fence posts, either. These were trees in among young hardwoods, which I wanted out of there.)

Then there are the future fence posts. During the year I planted one wet spot and one dry spot with young cedars brought up from a cousin's place in Connecticut. If all goes well, I'll be fencing with really classy posts in a few years.

Finally, I spent nearly half my 174 hours pruning up trees with a chainsaw, a pole saw, and forester's shears. Mostly these were red and white pines, which will one day be high-quality saw logs – or at least higher quality than if I hadn't pruned them. There were also immediate benefits: two or three cords of pine branches to use as sugar wood, and considerably more light in the new Bill Hill pasture. Slab wood from the mill is $15 a cord, so that's another $30 credit. Which brings the wood totals to 406 hours and $1,045.30.

MAPLE SYRUP. In 1977 I made 57 gallons, and spent 142 hours doing it. A lot of this went to friends and relatives. ('It's awful easy stuff to give away,' the man who taught me how to sugar once observed.) Some went as pay to neighbors whose trees I had tapped. We kept 6 gallons ourselves. But I still sold 29 gallons of syrup and 6 pounds of maple sugar, for a gross price of $417. My expenses for cans, etc., came to $106.39, which means the profit amounted to $310.61.

For the six gallons we used ourselves, I can count either the $34 that that much Log Cabin would have cost, or the $75 we would have spent if we had gone out and bought that much maple syrup. Since I don't use Log Cabin, I will naturally count the $75.

Meanwhile, another glance at the gross national product. A gallon of maple syrup contains precisely seven pounds of sugar. So this year we made 399 pounds of sugar. Over the past few years we've made a ton and a half. The average American is said to eat 87 pounds of sugar a year. It is pleasant to reflect that so far I have produced my own entire consumption from birth to age thirty-four. A few more years and I'll be caught up. Then we can start on the rest of the family.

HAY. During the summer I put about two tons of loose hay in the barn. Worth at least $100. But as all of it got eaten by our horse during the winter, plus more hay we had to buy; and as the horse contributes nothing whatsoever to farm production, I will ignore both hay and horse, and pass quickly on.

SHEEP. In cooperation with our next-door neighbors, we raised 4 lambs. They cost $15 each (a bargain). Since they lived almost entirely on grass, and since we did the butchering ourselves, the only expenses were $6 for powdered milk the first month, $1.05 for a roll of freezer paper, and 80¢ for getting eight pounds of lambburger ground at the store. The total cost of our family's two lambs therefore came to $37.85. To buy two large fall lambs at a butcher shop would cost about $150. Net gain: $112.15.

It's hard to keep accurate records of how much time you spend taking care of a few sheep, because you spend it in dribs and drabs. Ten minutes with your daughters in the afternoon, giving each lamb a pop bottle full of milk when they are young. Half an hour moving the half-grown lambs from one pasture to another every couple of weeks. Five minutes taking them water every couple of days. The one large chunk of time was nine and a half hours slaughtering, butchering, and wrapping. I think a fair guess for the total would be thirty hours.

CIDER. We made 28 gallons of cider, and drank it all, except for 3 gallons we gave to a friend who helped me fix the press. There were no expenses, except 30¢ worth of gasoline taking the truck to and from the orchard. Since store cider cost $1.79 a gallon, we would have spent $44.75 buying that 25 gallons. Subtract the gas, and the farm gets a credit of $44.45.

But that's not all. After you press cider, you have a lot of squeezed apples left. Pomace, the stuff is called. Our twelve bushels of pomace went to Floyd Dexter's beef cattle. We got a couple of nice steaks in return, and I'll take an additional $5 credit for that.

Time? Twelve cider pressings took almost exactly twelve hours, and it took about two hours to gather the windfalls that we used.

OTHER APPLE PRODUCTS. For about three months in the fall of 1977 we had either apple pie or applecake several times a week, for a total of at least fifty pies and cakes. My wife feels we should not count her pie-making and our applesauce-making time, since there not only would have been as much with store apples, but a shade more. We would have washed any store apples we planned to use for applesauce, to make sure we weren't eating chemical spray by mistake. So what we do count is the nine hours (about half of it child time) it took to pick 22 bushels of cooking and eating apples. Plus one full day I spent pruning apple trees, and a couple of hours planting two new ones. For the 22 bushels of apples we didn't buy, we get a credit of $88, less $16 for the two new trees.

Add all this up and the grand total comes to 611 hours spent working the farm, and $1,664.51 worth of cash products. Plus a small but perceptible contribution to the balance of trade. Plus roughly $10,000 worth of amusement.

Part-time farmers *are* just playing. We have one of the most pleasurable occupations known to man. But even on a farm as lightly worked as mine, we also accomplish something. If you could see the part-time farm of my neighbor Gary Ulman, who must produce ten times what I do, you might even say a lot.

Making the Grass Grow Green

IN SPRING, according to Tennyson, a young man's fancy lightly turns to thoughts of love. This is a dubious proposition at best. A young man's fancy, like a young woman's, has probably been focused on such thoughts all winter, not to mention the preceding fall and summer, so how could it turn in the spring?

What *is* true, though, is that in the spring a farmer's mind heavily turns to thoughts of manure. The stuff has been piling up behind his barn all winter – or, rather, he has been laboriously piling it up there. Something on the order of four tons per cow. It was bad enough lugging it out every day for five months, but now he has to spread it. After the pile unfreezes and before the grass gets so long that his tractor will crush it, he has maybe a month. And a hundred spreader loads, maybe, to go into the fields.

Last spring I had an even bigger job than that. I had a literal mountain to move.

Eleven years ago I bought a field that used to go with the farm across the road. The previous owner, a New York lawyer, had sold the place, which meant kicking out the old tenant farmer who lived there. (To be fair, the old man had first refusal, but couldn't or wouldn't pay the lawyer's price.) The people from Connecticut who snapped the place up were mainly after the house, and proved willing to resell me the pasture. As Vermont pastures go, it was a quite level one. On one side, however, a long, narrow hill rose abruptly from the level grass. It was covered with rank weeds, including thistles the size of lilac bushes. This was the old farmer's manure pile.

For the last dozen years before he had to move, the tenant had faithfully wheeled infinite wheelbarrow loads of manure out of the barn, and out a little plank road to the end of the growing hill. But he had done no spreading at all. For one thing, he would have had to borrow his son's manure spreader, and his son lived three miles away, over the ridge. But mainly he had the feelings that any sane tenant farmer does. He wasn't about to kill himself improving someone else's fields.

When I came on the scene, the pile was about sixteen feet high, eighty feet long, and perhaps forty feet wide. I never even considered spreading it myself, having neither tractor nor manure spreader. I did dig out bits to use. Every year I put a couple of truckloads on my garden. Once, carried away by orchard fever, I spread a truckload in a neat ring around each of twenty-six apple trees. I freely allowed town friends to take as much as they cared to for their gardens. Sometimes they took one bushel basket, sometimes two. Once an ambitious young mother took fifteen burlap sackfuls – and nearly broke the springs in her station wagon. These various nibbles diminished the pile perceptibly but not radically – say, it shrank about one percent a year.

Meanwhile, I slowly discovered more and more disadvantages to having a manure mountain on the edge of the field. One was that it acted like a giant sponge, catching tons and tons of water during a rainy spell, and then gradually releasing it for weeks afterward. I have got my truck stuck in the mud on the farm road that went fifty feet below that manure pile at a time when you couldn't have got a Cadillac limousine stuck anywhere else on the farm. Another was that a cattle fence that goes up and over a manure mountain is less stable and more easily surmounted by cows than a cattle fence that just goes over regular ground.

But most important, that pile was an inexhaustible reservoir of weeds. I've mentioned that in its vicinity thistles grew six feet tall, and put out ten stalks from one root. Huge burdocks ringed the pile. Beggar's-lice grew all over it, mixed with nettles and motherwort. A chart of weed distribution in the pasture would have consisted of innumerable lines all pointing back to the manure pile, sort of the way the chart of an epidemic points back to the original disease carrier.

So when I finally did buy a tractor, one of my motives was to level that manure pile.

Even with a tractor you don't just drive out to a pile that might weigh somewhere between five hundred and a thousand tons, and wade in. First you need a plan. I had one. All my nibblings had been with an ordinary shovel, but now it was time for large-scale digging. So I had made a deal with Erni French that he'd come over with his tractor, which has a big bucket loader on the front. And I made a deal with Sam Farnham to borrow his son-in-law's manure spreader.

But it would be silly to have Erni there all day, loading the one spreader with his great steel-toothed loader and then sitting there doing nothing for ten or fifteen minutes while I spread the load out. So I also made a deal with Floyd Dexter to come over with *his* tractor and spreader. One deal involved a combination of money and grazing rights, one involved maple syrup, and one was a labor trade.

On the morning of May 24th, just about nine o'clock, when morning chores were done, a procession of tractors and spreaders entered the field. The cows, wild with curiosity, followed us over to the manure mountain, snorting and throwing their hind legs in the air and pretending to be scared. They knew my tractor by now, but Floyd's and Erni's were new to them, and cows love to find a menace in new equipment.

Erni drove straight to the steep front edge of the pile and took a trial bite. His bucket came up with what would have taken me half an hour to load by hand. Floyd brought his tractor and spreader around in a circle, so as to get the spreader exactly in front of and at right angles to Erni. The loading began.

Making the Grass Grow Green

All the rest of that day and half of the day after, there was constantly one tractor and spreader loading, and one out in the fields laying ancient but still aromatic manure in swath after swath. It looked, my wife tells me, like a motorized scene from Brueghel. If so, she herself supplied the final artistic touch, coming out with our youngest daughter and a two-quart can of lemonade in midafternoon. (The beer that we also drank Floyd had brought along in the cab of his pickup.)

When we all turned our tractors off and quit, about two in the afternoon on May 25th, the pile was four-fifths gone. Both pastures were fully dressed, and I had even taken a few loads around to the new piece of grazing behind Bill Hill.

We stopped partly because if we had taken even one more load we might have collapsed the cattle fence that climbed up and over the remaining end of the pile. It would be easier to deal with the fence later, when the cattle weren't right there, looking over our shoulders. And partly because the fields just didn't need any more fertilizing, and it made sense to save the rest for next year.

Old manure is not so rich as new manure. But it is still good stuff. The grass was greener and the cattle were fatter than any year since I've been here. The weed infection has stopped. Spreading the wealth may or may not be a good idea with money, but it's a terrific idea with fields.

Ten Ton of Stun

ANYONE WHO OWNS LAND IN VERMONT has rocks to deal with. Anyone who both owns land and farms it becomes a specialist in rocks. He has to. Rocks are natural enemies of farm equipment. A boulder sticking up as little as two inches can catch your cutter bar when you're mowing hay – and few thuds are more sickening. Hitting, say, five rocks in the course of an afternoon's mowing can reduce a man to quivering jelly. I have known a sober middle-aged farmer to leap off his tractor and peer through the tall grass like Tarzan tracking elephants, because he thought he caught a glimpse of a gray hump in the next swath.

Stones in plowland are even worse. No worry about the ones above ground; here you can easily see them, and, at some cost to the straightness of your furrows, detour around. But the ones just under the surface are another matter. You fear that at any second the plowshare will smash into one. A Vermonter plowing a strange field consequently wears the cautious expression of a pilot guiding a ship into a harbor that he knows to be full of shoals and reefs and quite possibly minefields.

For these reasons, a good farmer will go to quite a lot of trouble to get the stones out of his fields. I myself am not a good farmer. Oh, I've pulled a few boulders out with my tractor, loaded them onto a borrowed stoneboat, and dragged them to the nearest swamp. I've even incorporated a few into stone walls. But I only attack the little ones – say, up to a thousand pounds.

The big ones I learn to avoid when I mow. As for plowing, I don't do any. I'm too chicken.

I have a young neighbor, though, who shows signs of becoming one of the best farmers around. For the last several years Ellis has been growing corn on a four-acre piece of plowland that his father and grandfather worked before him. It's good land, too: level and well watered.

Long ago – probably in the eighteenth century – some farmer took out all the stones that could be moved with a team of oxen. More recently, Ellis's father got some still bigger ones with his tractor. What that left was a beautiful clear field with about eight giant boulders dotted across it, ranging in size from half a Honda to a whole Chevy II. Some were half out of the ground, some nearly flush. A couple more lurked five or six inches under the surface, with soil carefully built up over them by Ellis's father and grandfather, the way a balding man combs his hair over the bald spot. From my point of view, those rocks were as enduring a part of our local landscape as Potato Hill, or the Pompanoosuc River.

One Sunday last August, though, I was walking past Ellis's cornfield on my side of the boundary and I noticed a scene of unusual activity. There were a tractor, a backhoe, and a little bulldozer gathered around one of the boulders. They weren't messing up the corn, because last year Ellis planted corn only on the upper side of the field, where there are no rocks. Naturally, I stopped to watch.

The backhoe had already dug a deep trench around the rock, which was one of the half-buried ones. And someone had already fixed slender logging chains around the rock, and the rock had visibly shifted forward in its bed.

At the moment I arrived, Ellis was sitting on his old Allis-Chalmers tractor, which was chained to the front of the rock. Ed Paige, his father, was beside him on the little bulldozer, similarly chained. A neighbor named Alford Stone, who's a professional equipment operator, had his backhoe to one side. By extending the boom as far as it would reach, Alford was just able to get the hoe teeth under the back of the rock. The tractor whined, the bulldozer growled and spun its worn treads, the backhoe made a throaty roar – and the rock moved forward in its hole maybe an inch.

Undismayed, Alford dismounted from his backhoe and jumped lightly onto the rock. 'We'll get this stun,' he said. He rearranged the chains so that the angle of pull would be slightly different. Then the tractor whined, the bulldozer growled, the backhoe roared. The rock crept forward and up out of the hole almost a foot.

Twenty minutes later, the rock was half out of the hole, and apparently coming no farther. The last two pulls hadn't moved it at all. Alford only smiled. He got Ed to take his place on the backhoe, and hopped on the bulldozer (which he owns). Ellis unchained it, and Alford calmly backed it down what looked to me like a sixty-degree slope into the bottom of the now quite large pit behind the rock. There was just room for it. He set the blade against the back of the rock, and once again every machine strained to the limit. The rock moved about half an inch.

'Maybe you could use another tractor,' I said to Ellis, and he agreed that another one could do no harm. It took me less than ten minutes to come snorting back on my International Harvester 504. Alford chained me to the front, next to Ellis. Then all four of us, mounted on our machines, pulled and pushed, and the great rock came lurching out of its hole.

No one broke out any champagne. Instead, Ed, Ellis, and Alford set about making a train. It had two engines, one car, and a caboose. First came Ellis's tractor, tightly chained to the bulldozer blade. Then the bulldozer, tightly chained to the rock. Then the boulder itself, looking enormous now that it was all above ground. Finally the backhoe, which Alford had turned around, so that now his bucket loader was pressed against the back of the rock.

Instead of someone blowing a whistle, Ed shouted, 'Let's go,' and the train moved off on a hundred-yard journey to a piece of

wet ground at the bottom of the field. There the boulder was pushed up against four others they had already taken out. The crew, not knowing anything about railroad rules on what constitutes a day's work, immediately set out on the next run.

Two days later, on my way out to my woodlot, I took a steel tape and measured the stone I had helped to pull out. It is nine feet long by eight feet wide, and at the center nearly four feet thick. Solid granite. Granite weighs 165 pounds per cubic foot. Making full allowance for irregularities and thin places near the edges, I calculate that boulder at well over ten tons.

Talk about weight lifters! Vermont farmers may well be the national champions.

Falling for Apples

THE NUMBER OF CHILDREN who eagerly help around a farm is rather small. Willing helpers do exist, but many more of them are five years old than fifteen. In fact, there seems to be a general law that says as long as a kid is too little to help effectively, he or she is dying to. Then, just as they reach the age when they really could drive a fence post or empty a sap bucket without spilling half of it, they lose interest. Now it's cars they want to drive, or else they want to stay in the house and listen for four straight hours to The Who. That sort of thing.

There is one exception to this rule. Almost no kid that I have ever met outgrows an interest in cidering. In consequence, cider making remains a family time on our farm, even though it's been years since any daughter trudged along a fencerow with me, dragging a new post too heavy for her to carry, or begged for lessons in chainsawing.

It's not too hard to figure out why. In the first place, cidering gives the child instant gratification. There's no immediate reward for weeding a garden (unless the parents break down and offer cash), still less for loading a couple of hundred hay bales in the barn. But the minute you've ground and pressed the first bushel of apples, you can break out the glasses and start drinking. Good stuff, too. Cider has a wonderful fresh sweetness as it runs from the press.

In the second place, making cider on a small scale is simple enough so that even fairly young children – say, a pair of nine-year-olds – can do the whole operation by themselves. Yet it's also picturesque enough to tempt people of any age. When my old college roommate was up last fall – and we've been out of college a long time – he and his wife did four pressings in the course of the weekend. They only quit then because I ran out of apples.

Finally, cider making appeals to a deep human instinct. It's the same one that makes a housewife feel so good when she takes a bunch of leftovers and produces a memorable casserole. At no cost, and using what would otherwise be wasted, she has created something. In fact, she has just about reversed entropy.

Cidering is like that. You take apples that have been lying on the ground for a week, apples with blotches and cankers and bad spots, apples that would make a supermarket manager turn pale if you merely brought them in the store, and out of this unpromising material you produce not one but two delicious drinks. Sweet cider now. Hard cider later.

The first step is to have a press. At the turn of the century, almost every farm family did. They ordered them from the Sears or Montgomery Ward catalogue as routinely as one might now order a toaster. Then about 1930 little presses ceased to be made. Pasteurized apple juice had joined the list of American food-processing triumphs. It had no particular flavor (still hasn't), but it would keep almost indefinitely. Even more appealing, it was totally sterile. That was the era when the proudest boast that, let's say, a bakery could make was that its bread was untouched by human hands. Was touched only by stainless-steel beaters and stainless-steel wrapping machines.

Eras end, though, and the human hand came back into favor. One result: in the 1970s home cider presses returned to the market. They have not yet returned to the Sears catalogue, but they are readily available. I know of two companies in Vermont that make them, another in East Aurora, New York, and one out in Washington state. If there isn't someone making them in Michigan or Wisconsin, there soon will be. Prices range from about 175 to 250 dollars.

Falling for Apples

Then you get a couple of bushels of apples. There *may* be people in the country who buy cider apples, but I don't know any of them. Old apple trees are too common. I get mine by the simple process of picking up windfalls in a derelict orchard that came with our place. I am not choosy. Anything that doesn't actually squish goes in the basket.

With two kids to help, collecting takes maybe twenty minutes. Kids tend to be less interested in gathering the apples than in running the press, but a quiet threat of no-pickee, no-pressee works wonders. Kids also worry about worms sometimes, as they scoop apples from the ground – apples that may be wet with dew, spiked with stubble, surrounded by hungry wasps. Occasionally I have countered with a short lecture on how much safer our unsprayed apples are than the shiny, wormless, but heavily sprayed apples one finds in stores. But usually I just say that I have yet to see a worm in our cider press. That's true, too. Whether it's because there has never been one, or whether it's because in the excitement and bustle of grinding you just wouldn't notice one little worm, I don't dare to say.

As soon as you get back with the apples, it's time to make cider. Presses come in two sizes: one-bushel and a-third-of-a-bushel. We have tried both. If I lived in a suburb and had to buy apples, I would use the very efficient third-of-a-bushel press and make just under a gallon at a time. Living where I do, I use the bigger press and make two gallons per pressing, occasionally a little more.

The process has two parts. First you set your pressing tub under the grinder, line it with a pressing cloth, and start grinding. Or, better, your children do. One feeds apples into the hopper, the other turns the crank. If there are three children present, the third can hold the wooden hopper plate, and thus keep the apples from bouncing around. If there are four, the fourth can spell off on cranking. Five or more is too many, and any surplus over four is best made into a separate crew for the second pressing. I once had two three-child crews present, plus a seventh child whom my wife appointed the official timer. We did two pressings and had 4¼ gallons of cider in 43 minutes and 12 seconds. (Who won? The second crew, by more than a minute. Each crew had one of our practiced daughters on it, but the second also had the advantage of watching the first.)

As soon as the apples are ground, you put the big pressing plate on and start to turn the press down. If it's a child crew, and adult meddling is nevertheless tolerated, it's desirable to have the kids turn the press in order of their age, starting with the youngest: at the end it takes a fair amount of strength (though it's not beyond two nine-year-olds working together), and a little kid coming after a big one may fail to produce a single drop.

The pressing is where all the thrills come. As the plate begins to move down and compact the ground apples, you hear a kind of sighing, bubbling noise. Then a trickle of cider begins to run out. Within five or ten seconds the trickle turns into a stream, and the stream into a ciderfall. Even kids who've done it a dozen times look down in awe at what their labor has wrought.

A couple of minutes later the press is down as far as it will go, and the container you remembered to put below the spout is full of rich, brown cider. Someone has broken out the glasses, and everybody is having a drink.

This pleasure goes on and on. In an average year we start making cider the second week of September, and we continue until early November. We make all we can drink ourselves, and quite a lot to give away. We have supplied whole church suppers. One year the girls sold about ten gallons to the village store, which made them some pocket money they were prouder of than any they ever earned by baby-sitting. Best of all, there are two months each year when all of us are running the farm together, just like a pioneer family.

In Winter in the Woods

A FARMER'S WORLD CONTRACTS in the winter to little more than his barn and his woodlot. Because I had no cows in my barn last winter, and hence no warmth, mine shrank to just the woodlot. The barn was still there, loaded to the gills (truck, tractor, many ranks of firewood, even a car we were storing for a friend), but bitterly cold. Even on sunny days no one ever went in it except to get firewood or start the tractor. When I felt the desire to hang around a barn and be comfortable, I went over to my neighbor Floyd's. There the two milkers and the eight beef cattle keep the temperature a comfortable sixty-five and the humidity high. The pigs are stretched out on their stomachs in their pen, like tourists on the beach in Florida, and Floyd's new black calf is over in a corner waiting to have her neck tickled. That barn is a little piece of summer.

But on my own farm nothing stirs except in the woods. There the deer plod through the snow at night, and I do by day. I cut trees; they come as soon as it is dark to eat the buds.

You see the woods quite differently in winter woodcutting than you do in any other activity or at any other time of year. There is a simplicity and even an abstractness to the scene. The grays and gray browns of tree trunks, which you would hardly notice in spring, summer, or fall, now leap at your eye. A green-needled hemlock is visible a hundred yards away, as conspicuous as a girl in a green raincoat would be on a Florida beach. The snow has covered all the ferns and briers and trailing cedar, so that the floor is the plainest possible white-on-white. Apart from your own clumsy tracks, there is a slim deer trail running from fallen treetop to fallen treetop, where they eat the buds you have made available. There is a lightly embossed pattern of rabbit tracks and what you guess to be red-squirrel tracks. Nothing else.

Or, rather, nothing else on cloudy days. On sunny days there is one thing more. On sunny days the snow gradually turns from pale gold to yellow gold as noon approaches, and then gradually fades again. By three o'clock on a January afternoon it is the palest of ash blonds. And then it happens. A faint rose color begins to appear. Slowly it gets stronger until just as the sun sets the whole floor is lightly but clearly washed with pink. Pink snow, with white showing through, and blue-gray shadows of the tree trunks and the rabbit tracks.

This whole scene ought to be available to skiers, except that skiers don't much go in the woods. Out on the open slopes there is too much glare, and not enough shadow. It ought to be available to snowmobilers, except that they're going too fast . . . and like all drivers, they have to keep their eyes on the road. It probably *is* available to snowshoers — when they're not too busy wiping the sweat from their eyes.

Except when I'm chainsawing, the scene is as quiet as it is simple. My winter woodlot may be the quietest place I've ever been. There are no leaves on the trees to rustle. There are no songbirds. Once in two weeks, maybe, a flock of chickadees will come check out the operation, but their bit of noise isn't *song,* and they only stay a few minutes anyway. Once in three winters, maybe, a woodpecker will discover that there are lots of freeze-dried ants available when I split red maples that are beginning to rot in the center, and will hang around for a month or more. But mostly woodpeckers dislike the rival noise of the chainsaw, and except that third winter it is rare to hear their rat-tat-tating. I never hear the deer or the rabbits, and the squirrels don't scold.

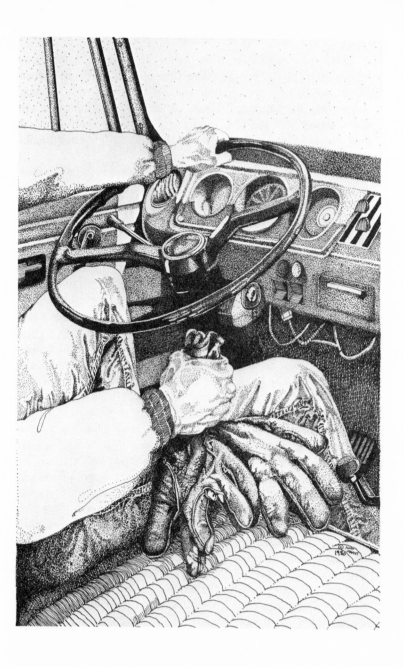

There is a road down in the valley. In fact, it's a numbered Vermont highway. But I seldom hear traffic. There isn't much in the middle of a winter afternoon, and what there is, is likely to be going slower than that same car or truck would in summer. On a snowy day the road might as well not be there at all. A few cars may go by, less than half a mile away, but the silence is total.

Only twice in all these years have I come on a scene of activity in the frozen woods. (I do not count the snowy woods of March, when two or three times I've stumbled onto a sugar camp with people gathering buckets and someone tending the evaporator.) One was a dozen years ago, when I was doing a kind of timber cruise at the very back of my land, and came on a small deer-yard. There were six deer in it, and no wind to warn them. As I arrived on one side, they exploded out the other. But except for the warning snort that the first deer that saw me gave, even that was a quiet scene. They might have been deer in a silent movie.

The other was last winter. I was cutting a red maple maybe twelve inches in diameter. Usually they don't begin to rot at the heart until they're larger than that, so I was surprised when the chainsaw began cutting fast and hurling out dark chips. Better get over here, woodpecker, I thought; there're going to be frozen ants. I was wrong. There were animals, if small ones. I was actually cutting into someone's peaceful barn.

That little maple was hollow at the bottom, and a family of deer mice were spending the winter in the hay-lined hollow. As soon as the tree fell, a little whiskered face poked up from the stump. The mouse saw me, and took a flying leap into the snow. But then where was there for him to go? A second later another mouse sprang out, and another. The air seemed to be full of deer mice. And then the snow was. Not only the three leapers, but two more mice, a little woozy from the shock of the fall, who ran out from holes in the trunk, now lying on the ground. None of them knew what to do next.

Deer mice are among the most charming of all rodents, with

their fawn-colored coats and white feet. I had two daughters and an empty gerbil cage at home. Without even stopping to think, I started catching mice. In that soft, deep snow it was easy to grab one. But once I'd caught him, then what? I had to get him out of the woods, into my truck, and a mile home while I drove. At first it seemed impossible. Then I thought of my gloves. I wound up leaving the woods bare-handed, with a mouse riding inside each glove. (As I found out when I got home, each had retreated to the thumb.) I drove with one hand, and held both gloves tightly at the cuff with the other. With the temperature about ten above zero, it was a chilly trip. I have tried to avoid cutting hollow trees since then, not for my hands' sake but because I don't like hurting other people's barns.

Those two days were exceptional. There have been hundreds of other days in the winter woods when I was alone with the sun, the snow, the shadows, and the trees. There is no more peaceful place. A Vermont woodlot is a little cold, and the days are short, but I'll take it over lying on a Florida beach any time.

Best Little Woods Tool Going

I LEARNED A LOT OF WOODCRAFT when I was a boy. Between the Boy Scouts, my father (a fine woodsman condemned to spend most of his life at a desk in New York City), the books of Ernest Thompson Seton, and the L. L. Bean catalogues with which our house was constantly awash, I knew my way around for a suburban kid. I could make a fire on a wet day, find east by looking at the top twigs of young hemlocks, space my chopping cuts accurately on a birch log twelve inches in diameter, and so on.

Among other things, I knew a fair amount about woods tools. This was the pre-chainsaw age (at least among Eastern sportsmen: I guess a few loggers were already staggering around with the early two-man models), but axes, hatchets, saws, and wedges were familiar objects almost from birth. By the time I was twelve, I could make a straight cut with a one-man crosscut, or pull lightly and smoothly on one end of a two-man saw – especially when my father was on the other end. I could place the splitting wedges with moderate accuracy in a knotty beech log. I had views on the weight of axheads. Give me a sharp bucksaw, and I would make you a fast pile of stovewood.

I had never heard of peaveys.

The peavey is an instrument worth hearing of. I won't say they're indispensable for the casual tree cutter – but they do make work in the woods a lot handier. The bigger the trees you fell, the handier a peavey is. Anyone who gets firewood from trees much over a foot in diameter could use one. Anyone who cuts even an occasional sawlog could use two.

Archimedes once boasted that if he had a long enough lever, he could move the world. Archimedes would have loved peaveys. A peavey can be defined as a lever with a built-in fulcrum. It consists of a heavy wooden handle three to four feet long, with a steel head. Mounted on one side of the head is a steel hook that will bite into a log. In this form it has existed for a very long time – lumbermen in classical Greece may have used bronze-headed ones, for all I know – and this primitive version is called a cant hook or cant dog. Then in 1858 a Maine blacksmith named Joseph Peavey got the idea of turning the fixed hook into a swinging hook that will bite easily into a log of any size. Eureka! The peavey.

I was around thirty when I saw my first peavey in action, and I wasn't very impressed. What I saw was a Connecticut farmer using one in its commonest and humblest function, to roll a log over. I had an Abercrombie and Fitch reaction. Or perhaps the same reaction a cross-country skier has when he sees his first snowmobile. The damned things just weren't sporting. I knew how to roll a log over; my father had taught me. What you do is to leave the stub of one branch when you're limbing – say, a stub three to four feet long – and then you just roll the log over with that. Organic log handling, so to speak.

A few years later I went out and bought a peavey. (You can get one for as little as fifteen or twenty dollars; the best big ones from Snow and Nealley, Bangor, Maine, might cost thirty dollars.) These days I own two. What happened in the interim was that I made the definite switch from crosscuts and axes to the chainsaw, and I had gradually begun to cut much larger trees than I ever did before.

The particular large tree that led me to buy my first peavey was a white ash growing in a fence line between two fields. Two and a half feet in diameter, and probably sixty feet tall. I wanted it out of there, partly because a couple of nice ten-inch sugar maples were growing practically under it, and I wanted them to have the light. But mostly because I needed some firewood in a hurry, and ash doesn't need much drying. (Though, as I discovered, it will burn a lot better if you *do* dry it.)

In my old crosscut days, dealing with that tree would have been a half-a-week project. An ash that size has two cords of wood in it, and weighs three tons. In fact, I might have just looked at it respectfully, and found something smaller. But by now I was fairly competent with a chainsaw. I strolled out and started cutting.

In a couple of hours I had the tree down and the whole top converted into firewood. Then it was time to attack the trunk. Since there were no limbs for the first thirty feet, I didn't have much limbing to do. In ten minutes I had the trunk bare (except, of course, for the turning stub I had left), and in another twenty I had all my cuts made partway through the trunk. Now to turn.

I gave the stub a firm push. Nothing at all happened. After a while I got my wife, and we both pushed. We couldn't even rock it much.

I have a standard procedure I use in such contretemps. It may lack macho prestige, but it works. I have three friends in town – two native, one not – who are clever at solving problems, and what I do is I call one of them. This particular day I called Tom Pinder, because I happened to know he was home putting a new roof on his house. (I did have the grace to wait until I knew he'd be in the house having lunch.) He came right over, bearing his peavey. He set the hook confidently, just about half-way up the trunk, and pushed. It *was* a big tree, and he did have to strain a bit, but it rolled obediently over. The next day I owned a peavey myself.

Loggers, as I understand, routinely use their peaveys to do everything but pick their teeth. Or at least they used to. There was even supposed to be one cook on the old Penobscot drives who stirred the big kettle of baked beans with a peavey. For the first few months I used mine only to roll logs. Then one day I made a mistake cutting a fifteen-inch red maple and got it hung up in a neighboring oak. I've lodged a good many trees, one time and another, and I am very familiar with the dangerous and humiliating business of cutting short sections off the bottom of the lodged tree and then hopping aside as the now unsupported top thumps down a few feet. I've even pushed a few very small lodged trees over by brute force.

But this one was far too big for me to push over, and it was still so nearly vertical that the idea of cutting a piece off the butt made me nervous. I've seen a man on whom a tree fell.

Once in a while I get an idea of my own. I got one now. Holding my peavey horizontally, I set the hook into the leaning tree about three feet up, and rotated it. The maple majestically spun like a giant top, came clear of the oak, and crashed on down right where I meant to have it in the first place. Thousands of loggers, I now know, have been doing the same for the last 122 years – but for me it was a true eureka moment.

There's a third thing I have learned to do with peaveys that is even more gratifying than the first two. This is to use them in low-technology log loading.

Maybe once a year I get an urge to cut a few white pines or wild black-cherry trees and have them sawed into lumber. Since Gary Ulman's sawmill is only two miles away, it's an urge I can gratify. But no one with a logging truck is going to come pick up my miserable four or five logs – or, at least, if someone did, it would cost so much that my boards would wind up more expensive than first-quality four-sides-planed stuff at the most expensive lumberyard in the Boston suburbs. Instead I take them over in my pickup.

But how do you get twelve-foot sawlogs off the ground and into the back of a pickup? There are various ways. Enough helium balloons will do it, or a forklift truck, or any of the larger-model helicopters. On one memorable occasion, I had six Dartmouth freshmen out for a picnic and got their help. Seven people can lift quite a heavy log, hard though it is for human arms to get a grip. A much simpler method, though, is to get one friend and equip him or her with your spare peavey. Then you back the pickup up to the smaller end of the log. One of you stands on either side of the log, and you hook on with your peaveys. You can get a splendid grip with the peavey, and the two of you can load it with ease. You have to expect a few grins, of course, when you trundle in to a sawmill with four small logs on a pickup – but I *have* known a real logger who was there with his monster truck and fifty big logs and cherry picker to get so involved helping me unload that he almost walked off with my spare peavey. I think he was having a fit of nostalgia.

Not that that's the only way to load logs with a peavey. That's just the way you do it when you've got a pickup and have to slide them in through the tailgate. With a more versatile truck, namely one that has removable sides, you can roll them on.

I did my first roll-on loading just about a year ago. I had gotten carried away and dropped a couple of white pines that even an Oregon logger wouldn't have sneered at. I don't say he'd have been *impressed*, but he wouldn't have called them Vermont toothpicks, either. They were nice tall pines, each with three sawlogs. The butt log of the bigger one was just about twenty inches in diameter. There's no way two people are going to pick up one end of a log like that and hoost it into the back of a pickup.

Fortunately, my neighbor George deNagy has an old one-ton farm truck, the kind that looks much bigger than it is because the bed sits up over the wheels. Except that it gets five miles to the gallon and won't start in cold weather, it's a lovely vehicle. And, of course, you can take the sides off.

George loves challenges. He was glad to come rumbling into my woodlot (that's no cliché – farm trucks invariably rumble; it's because of those detachable sides) and pull up next to my modest log pile. We then cut three ten-foot hemlock saplings. Two are all you really need; the third is just a little piece of insurance in case you've cut the saplings too small and one of them happens to break just as you're rolling a log up.

We laid the saplings against the side of the truck so as to form a ramp. One went at each end of the truck bed, and the insurance sapling rested in the middle. Then we hooked on to the first and biggest log with our peaveys and began to roll. It worked beautifully. The bark on a green sapling makes a nice corrugated surface, and the log never even threatened to slip. (I'm told that people who use sawed timbers for the ramp sometimes find the log skidding right back down onto their feet.) In twenty minutes we had loaded all six logs and were on our way to Gary's mill. Two weeks later I had as handsome a pile of clear pine lumber as a man could ask for. Score another victory for the peavey.

I have probably now reached my personal limit of peavey skills. After all, I started late. But there is one other of their many uses that I hope to witness sometime in my life. Peaveys are the tool of choice in river drives. I once heard a lumberjack's song about breaking a logjam. The boss wanted to dynamite it – which of course would have damaged some of the logs, besides being crude and noisy – and the lumberjacks said no, they could pick it apart. Guess with what. As the song put it:

> *But before you try the powder,*
> *Or to break her with the juice,*
> *Hand some peaveys to the river rats and jacks.*
> *They will roll her and they'll crowd her*
> *And they'll break the timber loose;*
> *Yes, they'll break her, or half a hundred backs.*

As poetry that's on the weak side, but as a vision it's something else. Fifty men out on a river with peaveys, swarming over a million board feet of tangled pine logs would be a sight worth seeing. If gasoline goes enough higher, I might even get to.

Maple Recipes for Simpletons

THERE ARE A LOT OF MAPLE RECIPES in existence. Someone once gave me a book that contains at least three hundred – in fact, that's all the book *does* contain. There are recipes for Maple-Cheese Spoon Dessert, and for Modern Maple-Pumpkin Pie. For baked squash covered with crushed pineapple and doused with maple syrup. For peanut-butter cookies. Even directions for a truly revolting salad dressing. (You mix cream and lemon juice, and then add a big slug of maple syrup. Oil and vinegar with a discreet touch of garlic is more my idea of a salad dressing.)

I yield to no one in my admiration for maple syrup. I've been making it for fifteen years; and even with my little rig, total production now comes to many hundred gallons. I have gradually learned to make not only syrup, but tub sugar, maple candy, and finally, just in the last few years, the highest art of all: granulated maple sugar that pours as readily as the white stuff you get in a five-pound bag at the store. These products taste, if anything, even better as the years go by.

But all the same, I view most maple recipes with dark suspicion. Too many of them put a noble product to unworthy, not to say peculiar, uses. Many also ignore the fact that maple syrup currently costs about eighteen dollars a gallon, and is thus a pretty expensive sweetening agent.

Take those peanut-butter cookies. To make one batch requires half a pint of maple syrup, and all you wind up with is some-thing that tastes like sweet peanut butter. Ten cents' worth of cane sugar could handle that job – and it's just the sort of humble task cane sugar was born for. As for mixing syrup with crushed pineapple and plastering it on hunks of squash, I'd as soon mix twelve-year-old Scotch with diet Pepsi.

I certainly don't claim all maple recipes are like that. A good maple cake, maybe with some butternuts in the frosting, is one of the joys of life. And I've had a maple charlotte I would walk several miles to have again. These are splendid uses of syrup; the maple flavor comes out, if anything, enhanced. My only problem is that I am not personally competent to make either a cake or a charlotte.

However, there are some recipes that I *can* handle and that are maple-enhancing. I propose to share three of them. Two are my own discoveries, the third is a standard rural treat. All three are notably easy to prepare. In fact, they are so simple that any cook is going to regard the word *recipe* as absurdly out of place. So perhaps I should instead say, here are three good uses for maple syrup.

The first recipe is for Vermont baklava. Greek baklava (which came first by about five hundred years) is a many-layered pastry soaked in and fairly oozing honey. Vermont baklava is less com-plex. The ingredients are a loaf of good-quality white bread (homemade, Pepperidge Farm, Arnold, etc.) and a can of maple syrup. To prepare it, you take two slices of bread from the loaf and place them in your toaster. Set the toaster on medium. When the toast pops up, remove and place on a plate. Then cover each piece generously with maple syrup. Wait two to three minutes for it to soak in. The baklava is now ready for con-sumption.

Two important tips: On no account heat the syrup, and on no account butter the toast. It is essential that the only ingre-dients be white bread and room-temperature syrup.

I stumbled on the recipe for Vermont baklava about ten years ago, when I first became a commercial-syrup producer. People began to stop by my farm to buy syrup. I would ask them what grade they wanted; and naturally enough a fair number didn't even know there *were* grades. My usual impulse was to give them a sample of each grade. But straight syrup from a spoon is a little overwhelming, and I certainly wasn't going to fire up the stove and make a batch of pancakes for every visitor. One day it occurred to me to try toast. I omitted butter simply because we happened to be out. And I then discovered that toasted white bread is one of the great vehicles for maple syrup. One gets the full brilliance of the flavor – if you'll forgive the arty term – and one gets something else that I have never experienced elsewhere except in tasting partly finished syrup in an evaporator. Poured at room temperature over toast, maple syrup by itself seems to have the qualities of butter, along with its own characteristics. The dish thus recommends itself especially to those who love butter but avoid it on account of their fear of polysaturated fats.

May be made with Fancy, A, or B. Not suggested with Grade C.

The second recipe will be of interest only to those who like to eat sliced bananas and milk. And even within that already limited group, only to those who feel that sliced bananas and milk go much better with brown sugar than with white sugar.

I have felt thus since roughly the age of six. In those early years I was likely to have a base of cornflakes under the bananas and brown sugar; since about sophomore year of college I have omitted the cornflakes. They only get soggy, anyway.

The ingredients called for in the second recipe are one or more ripe bananas, a supply of whole milk, and some dark maple syrup. Slice the bananas in the usual way, add the normal quantity of milk, and then pour in a couple of tablespoons of maple syrup. (Right in the milk? You feel it might be like adding syrup to crushed pineapples and squash? I assure you it is not.)

The recipe is again one I stumbled on. One night a couple of years ago I happened to be fixing dinner alone. My wife and daughters had gone to a fair, and wouldn't be back until late. I usually figure on a maximum preparation time of ten minutes when I'm fixing dinner alone, so as to waste as little time as possible indoors. The menu this particular evening was a hamburger, to be followed by sliced bananas, milk, and brown sugar. Then I couldn't find the brown sugar. Not only no real brown sugar, but not even any of that light-tan stuff that will do in a pinch.

I already had the bananas sliced. Some kind of sweetening was necessary for the milk. We happened to have an open jar of Grade C in the pantry. I went and got it. At first bite I realized that for over forty years I had been having second-class bananas and milk. With brown sugar it's good. With dark maple syrup it's better.

May be made with Grade C or Grade B. Not recommended with Fancy or A.

The third recipe is the New England equivalent of sweet-and-sour pork in a Chinese restaurant, and it is a traditional spring dish. Warning: Anyone on a diet – in fact anyone who is not something of a glutton – should not even read about this dish.

Ingredients: a dozen plain raised doughnuts (two dozen, if more than four people will be present), a large jar of dill pickles, a quart or more of maple syrup.

First you boil the syrup down by about one-third, so that it has the consistency of a sugar glaze. Meanwhile, quarter the dill pickles and put them in a dish in the middle of the table, right next to the unsweetened raised doughnuts. Then, while it is still warm, you put some syrup in the bottom of a soup dish for each person.

Everybody then takes a doughnut, dips it in his or her bowl of syrup, and begins to gorge. After every two or three bites – or at a minimum twice per doughnut – you stop and eat a bite of pickle. With this constant resharpening of the palate, it is possible to eat an astonishingly large number of doughnuts. Stop just before you are comatose, and conclude with a cup of brewed coffee. Then retire to bed.

Should be prepared with Fancy or A. B will do, though not as well. C is not recommended.

This by no means exhausts the list of simple maple recipes – a small quantity of B or C does wonders in a pot of baked beans, a little A on popcorn beats Cracker Jack hollow. But it's enough to use as much spare syrup as most people are going to have in the course of a year.

There's a Phaeton in Your Future

L o n g a g o American cities were full of horses. The streets were filled with sleighs in the winter, and cabriolets, coaches, phaetons, and wagons the rest of the year. There was even horse public transit. Henry James describes one case of it in his novel *The Europeans*, which takes place in about the year 1845. A German baroness is looking out a window of 'the best hotel in the ancient city of Boston,' watching the horsecars go by, one every three minutes. She has never seen two horses pull such a big load (it's the trolley tracks that make it possible); and she has never seen such bright colors on a public conveyance, or heard so many harness bells. She is fascinated.

Those days, of course, are utterly gone. Gone beyond recall. Not even the oldest of Bostonians can remember the red-and-blue horsecars. It is three generations since any appreciable number of wagons rolled the streets. It is twenty years since the federal government even bothered to count the number of horses in America – though it continues to keep close tabs on automobiles, tractors, subway rolling stock, etc. Officially, a few mounted police are about all that's left.

Just after the government quit watching, though, something very strange happened. A trend of more than fifty years reversed itself. After declining steadily from about 1910 to 1963, the number of American horses began to inch back up. Then in the seventies it began to surge. By the best guesses, there were fewer than five million horses fifteen years ago. By the best guesses, there are almost nine million now. Much of that increase has taken place in the urban East. In states such as Massachusetts and New Jersey, the number of horses has nearly tripled.

Insofar as people are aware of this phenomenon at all, they tend to think it is caused entirely by fourteen-year-old girls. All fourteen-year-old girls, it is well known, read books about horses. Quite a large number will, if they can talk their parents into it, personally own a horse, which they will spend their days riding, grooming, and entering in shows. The theory is that nowadays fourteen-year-old girls simply have more indulgent (and more prosperous) parents, so that a higher proportion of them get to canter about on horseback, as opposed to merely dreaming about it.

If this theory were entirely correct, the impact of the horse boom on city life would be minimal. But it is not entirely correct. The horse boom certainly started with saddle horses, but it has now spread to include all kinds of horses. The number of big draft horses used in farming started to go up some years ago, in the Midwest as well as in New England. Most recently, the number of driving horses has started to increase. Driving horses are what you see in cities. A new horse age has begun.

One of the results of the resurgence in driving horses is that cabriolets, coaches, phaetons, and wagons are beginning to be made again. Virtually none were made for many years, because there was a huge glut of vehicles left over from the first horse age. I have four old sleighs in my barn at this minute, for example. They form a complete set for the well-run Vermont farm of 1920 – work sleigh, Sunday-go-to-meeting sleigh, teenagers' light runabout for courting, family sedan. Faced with millions of brand-new Model Ts on one side, and this glut of used equipment on the other, the great carriage makers like Abbot and Downing, of Concord, New Hampshire, folded up one by one. No one even cared. As recently as ten years ago, someone who wanted a horse-drawn vehicle would just pick up an old one for a song and restore it.

But for several years now, supply has not been equal to demand. Nowhere near equal. The result is that small carriage-making firms are springing up all over the country. To my certain knowledge, there are at least nine in operation.

One of these nine is about eighty miles north of Boston. It will soon be supplying the Eastern market, as Abbot and Downing once did. This is the Lincoln Buggy and Sleigh Works, of Contoocook, New Hampshire.

Lincoln Buggy and Sleigh does not look a bit like a Detroit automobile factory. The whole operation is housed in one large wooden building, which the workers (all three of them) put up before they started making vehicles. Out back is a ten-acre woodlot. One day, red-oak boards from that woodlot will be made into wagons. That they'll be air-dried on the spot rather than baked in a giant kiln at some far-off Weyerhaeuser plant is an actual advantage. Kiln-dried oak checks too much for use in horse-drawn vehicles.

There *is* an assembly line inside the building, but it is in no way an automated one. Joe Morette, the twenty-six-year-old brown-haired, brown-bearded owner of Lincoln Buggy and Sleigh, figures that a production run of three vehicles is needed for efficiency. So, at any given moment, three carriages of the same kind are in various stages of completion down the center of the shop. The last time I was there, he had three express wagons on the line – long, high wagons with elegant lines and big rear wheels. They are drawn by two horses. You could put benches in one and use it to run a local bus route, though more commonly they are used for fast freight service. One was just a body, sitting on a giant worktable. The next had its wheels on, and all its brass and bronze fittings. (These are produced in a homemade blacksmith shop at the end of the building.) The third was almost ready to ship. The purchaser – a woman who publishes a new and thriving magazine for draft-horse enthusiasts, called *The Evener* – had specified that it be painted Irish lavender, with bishop-purple trim. It looked terrific.

The next production Morette had in mind was three lady phaetons, one to go to Alaska, and after that three landaus, one of which was to go to the cosmetics firm of Estée Lauder.

There's a Phaeton in Your Future

Making horse-drawn vehicles seems to be not a job but a passion. For Joe and his wife, Linda ('her name is on the mortgage, too'), it has been a steady goal since they became adults. Joe's two part-time coworkers are equally committed. The younger one, Sheldon Cassiday, of Concord, New Hampshire, is part-time because he's still in the eleventh grade at Concord High School. Sheldon has a girlfriend who has a horse. A year ago, they started fixing up an old buggy for the horse to pull and found that one wheel was damaged beyond their skill to repair. (Presumably that was why the vehicle had been on the market.) They'd heard about the new buggy works in Contoocook and drove over. Sheldon took one look around and asked if he could become an apprentice.

The older coworker, Bill Arns, is part-time because he is a retired aircraft designer, living in Warner, New Hampshire. Bill now puts his mind to things like aluminum castings for experimental hubs on wagon wheels. He and Joe shared in the design of the phaetons, landaus, express wagons, and farm carts that they have made so far. And this summer Bill is personally going to deliver the lady phaeton that's going to Alaska.

In the country, it is already fairly common to see a buggy or a buckboard moving placidly along. It is even more common, in Vermont and New Hampshire, to see a big draft horse twitching logs out of the woods. Occasionally, one sees a pair of them pulling a farm wagon or a ground-driven manure spreader. I already have a neighbor who owns a spanking-new dumpcart made by Lincoln Buggy and Sleigh.

In the city, these changes are going to come more slowly. But I will still bet a nickel that within five years there will be new express wagons and phaetons rolling around the streets of a good many American cities. Not just for publicity, like the Budweiser horse teams or the Estée Lauder landau, but for normal transportation. The first horse age ended when horses lost out to the horseless carriage. The second will begin as cars and trucks start to lose out to the gasless carriage.

The Natives Are Restless

ONCE THERE WAS A YEAR when my mother, my ex-wife, and I were all maintaining households in the same small Vermont town. This made problems for the rural mail carrier. We have no street addresses in rural New England, and letters have to be sorted by name only. Not often, but once every couple of weeks the carrier would deliver a letter to the wrong one of us.

One Saturday I was in the general store, which also contains the post office. While I was there I returned a letter that should have gone to my ex-wife but had come to me. Lois Paige, the Saturday postmistress, apologized for the error. 'It's hard to keep the three of you straight,' she said a little defensively.

Lois is a very nice woman. At that time I had known her for ten years and had been joking around with her in a mild way for nine years. I joked around a little now. 'I don't see why it's so hard,' I said. 'After all, there are seven families of Fifields in town.'

'That's different,' she said quickly. 'They've always been here.'

Lois wasn't putting me down. She's too nice to do that. She was just explaining why three families of Perrins were hard for the post office, and seven families of Fifields were easy. In doing so she was carrying on a New England tradition at least two hundred years old. She was distinguishing between natives and outsiders.

The Natives Are Restless

In most parts of the world *native* is a term avoided by right-thinking people. It is used chiefly by colonial administrators, by tourists of the vulgar sort (who love to get pictures of the natives doing their quaint native thing), and by imperialist-fascist bastards ('You don't seriously argue that the *natives* could keep the canal operating!'). Historically, to 'go native' has been to lose one's civilized status.

In New England, on the other hand, 'native' is the condition that all of us newcomers aspire to. The more rural the part of New England, the truer this is. There's nothing specially glorious about being a native of, say, Worcester, Massachusetts, but to be a native of Dixville Notch, New Hampshire – that's a status worth having. Transplanted Californians and dropout Worcesterites who live in places like Dixville Notch dream of the day when they can stand up in town meeting and talk just like everybody else – or if that is not to be, the day their children can. They not only want to be accepted by the natives, they want to *be* natives. Meanwhile, the aspirant treasures moments such as the time this family from New York City came into the general store, mistook him for the proprietor, and tried to buy a pound of Crowley cheese.

The glory of nativehood is not even limited to human beings. Everything indigenous to rural New England shares in the glamour, right down to local foodstuffs. This is in striking contrast to the situation elsewhere. Once when I spent a few months working in Poland, I found that the American embassy had a kind of grocery store down in the basement, with tons of American canned goods, milk flown in from Denmark, and so on. The only Polish product in the whole store was fresh eggs, and even about them the manager was apologetic. But in New England an aura surrounds local produce. 'Native Corn' is one of the great boasts you can see on a sign. Native maple syrup has such cachet that at one time about half of all the syrup made in upstate New York was quietly shipped to Vermont, reheated, canned, and then sold as the real thing. A friend of mine once saw a store in a Maine village that had a sign in the window,

'Native Ice.' She never did figure out what rival store was selling imported ice.

All of this has been a very good thing. A mild superiority complex is probably the healthiest of all human conditions.

But in recent years there have been troubling signs. We outsiders still admire the natives, and still want to be like them. But there is mounting evidence that the natives want to quit being natives. The burden is too great.

I noticed an early sign of this change a few years ago when a classics professor and his French wife came to live in our village. Fairly soon after their arrival, the wife's mother and uncle came on a visit from Paris. The uncle was a small man with a big beret and a still larger movie camera.

For a solid month, he was all over the village with that camera. When Sunday service ended at the Methodist church, there he was by the door, Gauloise dangling from his mouth, getting footage of the twenty or so parishioners filing out. If the town road crew replaced a culvert, he was six feet away, taking mug shots. At first everyone just sort of ignored him. Plenty of tourists had taken pictures in the village before. But gradually the suspicion began to dawn on the villagers that they were, well . . . picturesque. They began to wonder uneasily if they were going to appear in some French version of *National Geographic*.

Before the month was over, the Methodists were coming out of the church at a dogtrot, their heads averted. No one actually held his hat over his face, like an old-time gangster leaving court, but there was clearly discomfort with our visiting *cinéaste*. The road crew took to fixing culverts on the far side of town. Self-consciousness had arrived.

Monsieur eventually went back to Paris. A year or two later the classics professor and his wife sold their house and moved in nearer to the college. Things went back to normal. Or so I thought.

Last year, though, I was involved in an incident that makes it clear that they are not back to normal, and probably never will be.

A young film maker named Richard Brick had come up from

New York to Chelsea, Vermont. Pretty soon he began making a movie about an old farmer who lived next door. It's the kind of movie that makes them drool in the suburbs – and authentic, to boot. Scenes of the old farmer, helped by a couple of even older friends, butchering his pig. Plowing with his ancient tractor. Complaining in his pure Vermont accent about the fierce rise in taxes. Taking his battered truck on a woods road you wouldn't suppose any vehicle could drive on. Leading the good life. If I didn't already live on a hill farm, that movie would have made me want to rush out and buy one.

The movie was sponsored by the Vermont Council on the Humanities and Public Issues; and last year I happened to be present when it was officially shown to a group of real Vermont farmers and their wives. The assistant state commissioner of agriculture was present to answer questions afterwards.

The showing was not a silent one. Audience participation was intense. A voice out of the darkness would mutter, 'Why did he have to pick a fellow that talks like my granddad?' Another voice would say, 'Look at that old tractor. Must be about a 'fifty-two. People are going to laugh at us.' A wife whispered reassuringly to her husband, '*No*, we're not quaint, Leon.'

When the lights came on, there was a torrent of questions. All of them fell into one of two categories: (1) Why the hell did the Vermont Council back a movie like that? (2) Would it be possible to get hold of all copies and burn them?

Then the farmers and their wives began to sketch out the kind of movie they would like to see made. The hero, it turned out, would be a man with two large modern tractors, no Vermont accent, and a farm that might just as well be in Iowa. As for his pretty wife, she would know nothing about pitchforks or putting down salt pork, and everything about computerized record keeping. The house inhabited by this up-to-date pair would probably feature a cocktail terrace where the two of them would sit and have a couple of martinis when they were finished with the evening milking. In short, just a couple of ordinary Americans.

To native-lovers like myself, this is all very alarming. New

England natives have not been ordinary; they have been a remarkable group. If they are about to quit on the job, then we need some more dropouts from Worcester to come in a hurry, and learn the accent (plus basic farming skills, such as how to drive workhorses and how to repair very old tractors) while there is still time. Rural New England without natives is unthinkable.

The Birds, the Bees, and the Cows

PART OF THE MYTHOLOGY about farm kids is that they
grow up very knowledgeable about sex. It's supposed to be from
watching the animals. Back at an age when all of us who grew up
in cities and suburbs were still wondering if it was true about
the stork, the myth says, farm kids were eagerly watching the
ram mount a few ewes, or sitting on the fence cheering the bull
on as he rode a cow, or hanging around the hen house while the
rooster feathered everything in sight.

So far as I can tell, the myth is almost wholly false. In the first
place, lots of farms these days don't *have* animals. Tractors, yes.
Bucket loaders, certainly. But not a stallion in sight. Nor any
mares, sows, boars, drakes, jacks, or ganders, either. In the second place, even when the farm has animals – a dairy farm, say –
it does not follow that much old-fashioned fun-to-watch breeding will take place. In fact, in the dairy world the technician
with his little tube of semen has largely replaced the bull – and
for both the cow and the onlooker the process is about as ex-
citing as getting a tetanus booster shot.

And even where a farm has plenty of animals of both sexes,
it still doesn't follow that the kids learn much. Farm animals are
remarkably discreet. It's domestic pets, such as people have in
the city, that lack inhibitions. A cocker spaniel thinks nothing of
having a meaningful encounter right in front of the TV set – and
lacking a bitch in heat (or a willing male, as the case may be),

is as likely as not to have a go at someone's trouser leg. The beasts of the field conduct their amours more privately. For the last three years, for example, we have had a sort of courting ground in the seven-acre pasture behind the house. A Hereford bull with testicles the size of cantaloupes has been here every summer all summer, running with anywhere between six and ten impressionable young cows. They have all duly had calves nine and a half months later. But none of my children has ever been present at *le moment critique*. At any of the numerous *moments critiques*, to be more accurate. Neither have I. I think he must handle all his affairs between three and six on cloudy mornings.

There is some visible sex on farms, of course. There is even a certain amount of kinky sex. For example, I am one of the very few people I know who has almost been raped by a cow. She wasn't even in heat at the time.

This cow was one of fourteen living in the pasture across the road, which is a pasture without a bull. All cows are curious (anytime you're doing something in a cow pasture, you wind up with an audience standing around you in a little circle to watch), and most are friendly. This particular cow, a two-year-old grade Holstein, was curious and friendly even beyond the norm. Any cow will come running up to people she knows, especially if she thinks there's a prospect of getting grain. This one would come up to strangers. If they stood still, pretty soon a big bovine head would be sniffing them all over. Soon after that, a long slate-colored tongue would come out, and give them an experimental lick. She might even try nibbling their clothes, just to see if by any chance they were good to eat.

My near-rape occurred once when I had a city-bred student out to the farm for the day. Naturally I had taken him over to be sniffed and licked (cows have sweet breath, and he had enjoyed it), and we were walking back toward the house. The whole herd was following us, just to be companionable, and the Holstein was, of course, the one closest behind. She always was. She liked to walk about two feet behind people.

Kendal and I were talking, and I wasn't paying much attention to our fourteen followers, when I suddenly got a feeling

of danger close behind. I looked around. The Holstein was standing up on her hind legs in the position of a bull about to mount his partner – which is also the position of a cow about to mount hers. Randy heifers sometimes do this to each other; it's known as 'bulling.'

Where she clearly meant to come down was on my shoulders. Even at that second, I knew she meant no harm. She was just a very affectionate cow. But as she weighed somewhere between 900 and 1,000 pounds, the least harm I could have hoped for would have been a couple of broken bones and a ruined back. I was able to sidestep just as she came crashing down – and from then on I carried a stick when I was in the pasture, and kept her at a distance. She never understood why.

Another cow in that same herd was involved in a similar incident about two months later, only this time as victim rather than aggressor. A pretty young heifer, mostly of Hereford blood, had come into heat. Cows do that about every three weeks. Some, especially the younger ones, advertise their state by letting out a series of loud, amorous moos. Around here it is usually referred to as 'bellering.' Whether they hope a passing bull will hear and come, or whether it is more like a serenade, I am not deep enough into cow psychology to say.

At any rate, this young Hereford was bellering her heart out. There were no bulls within easy hearing, but there *were* four black Angus steers. They were in an adjoining pasture used by my neighbor Ellis Paige.

No matter how young you castrate them, steers never quite forget that nature intended them to be bulls, and Angus are more stubborn and Scotch and tenacious of memory than most. They can also jump higher.

These four stood in a row, listening to the loud, yearning moos – and then the two older ones walked up to the barbwire fence. The young heifer flew up to the fence on my side. For some time she touched noses first with one steer and then the other. She bellered only occasionally, and then it was more like a croon.

The Birds, the Bees, and the Cows

Suddenly one of the two Angus wheeled around and marched about thirty yards back from the fence. He blew loudly through his nose and stamped the ground, just like a bull. Then, like a black racing car with legs, he came roaring toward the fence and leapt right over. Ten seconds later he had mounted the heifer.

Meanwhile, his friend backed up and tried the same maneuver, and he made it, too. One of the two younger steers, now wildly excited, made a run at the fence, lost his nerve at the last minute, and turned. Then he came thundering back, made no effort to jump, and simply crashed on through. The fourth followed through the gap.

All this time the first one was still riding the young heifer. There is no way steers can consummate these things, but sometimes they will keep trying all night. The heifer was a lot stronger than I am, and she had the advantage of four legs, besides. Even so, fifteen hundred pounds of steer on her back was beginning to feel a bit heavy, and she was trying to walk out from under him. He was preventing this by walking right along with her, using his rear legs only. (He was, of course, holding her tight with the front ones.) The other three steers were milling around, making tentative attempts to mount cows not in heat, and getting nowhere.

At this point three different farmers arrived, to try to separate the herds. It took more than an hour. The first time we got the Angus out, the two big ones simply came sailing over the fence again. In the end, the two herds had to be put in fields that didn't adjoin. By then, the poor little heifer was ready to swear off men for life. Or at the very least, until her next heat.

One of my daughters, incidentally, did see part of the Black Angus Raid; and she found it both educational and fascinating. I am told the story went all around the sixth grade the next day. I don't claim that farm kids never learn *anything* about the facts of life. Just not very much.

Neither of my children learned anything from the most interesting encounter I have seen on a farm, because neither of them was born yet. A couple of months before our elder daughter was born, my wife and I visited a horse-breeding farm owned by a cousin. It was Thoroughbreds that he raised, and there are no technicians or little tubes of semen used with Thoroughbreds. The stallions do it all.

But because a stallion can only cover maybe forty mares a year, and because each of these coverings is worth somewhere between 500 and 50,000 dollars, they do get some help* from other stallions. The other stallions are called teasers.

A mare from across the state arrived to be bred while we were there, and we got to watch. They put her in a large box stall, all by herself. In one wall there was a window about two feet square, shut with a wooden shutter. There seemed to be a lot of trampling and noise on the far side, where there was presumably another stall.

As soon as the mare was settled in, a groom came and opened the shutter. Immediately a horse's head and neck shot through the opening. This was the teaser, a good-looking palomino stallion.

He didn't waste a second. He reached out as far as he could, trying to give her what I think are called love bites. Meanwhile he kept up a continuous excited whinnying. My wife and I took it to mean something like 'Baby, if I could get through this damned window, I would mount you so fast . . .'

The mare at first didn't even permit him a nibble. She could easily keep out of his reach by staying on the far side of her stall. But she gradually moved over to the side with the window, and my wife swears she heard her giggle and say, 'Oh, Mr. Teaser, what strong teeth you have! And that blond mane is so cute!'

---

* This doesn't mean the stallion only copulates forty times a year. It's more like a hundred. He just confines himself to forty partners. What the mare's owner gets for that enormous stud fee is a guaranteed pregnancy – and if a mare does not conceive after the first covering, the stallion bravely tries again. Occasionally he may meet the same mare as many as seven times – and see her again next year, too.

The Birds, the Bees, and the Cows

At this point two grooms came and led her out into a court-yard. (The palomino nearly squeezed through that little window as he saw her leave – and then we could hear a drumbeat as he started to kick the walls.)

Out in the courtyard the real stallion was waiting. He didn't say a word. He just got right on and earned his 3,000 dollars in about fifteen seconds, while palomino drums played in the distance. My wife, who worries about the psychic welfare of all living creatures, was relieved to hear that once or twice a year the poor teaser usually gets to cover some local farm mare. (It doesn't spoil him for his work even those one or two days. He is so permanently frustrated that half an hour after the local mare has left, he is ready to promise anything to a highborn visitor in the next stall.)

But that's high drama on a stud farm. On ordinary farms, we hardly notice the affairs of the animals from one month to the next. Just how casually we take it all can be expressed by an incident that happened the first year I ever owned beef cattle. I had two: a heifer I was going to sell and an eighteen-month-old Hereford bull I was going to butcher.

Along in September, a couple of months before we planned to beef him, a man came to the door. 'Been lookin' at that little bull,' he said to my wife (I was at work). 'I like his lines. Don't suppose you want to sell him?'

My wife said no, we were going to put him in the freezer.

'Now that's a real pity,' the man said. 'Let me tell you what I want him for. I've got six heifers I want to breed. 'Course I could use this here artificial in-semi-nation. But you do that, you got to watch and see when each one comes in heat. I ain't real interested. But' – and here he nodded out toward the pasture – '*he* would be.'

That's how we are in the country. We just ain't real interested.

Vermont Silences

THERE IS AN OLD STORY about two Vermont farmers
who lived a mile apart – one west of the village, and the other
east of it. Since rural free delivery didn't exist yet, each had to
come into town to get his mail. Every weekday for twenty
years Eben would finish morning milking and come striding into
the village from the west, while Alfred did the same thing from
the east. Since both were punctual men, they invariably met in
front of the post office at nine a.m., just as the last letters were
being put up. They'd say good morning, go in and get their
mail, and stride off home – one west and one east.

One morning during the twenty-first year, however, Eben
came stumping out of the post office and, ignoring his usual
route, started briskly south, down the state highway. Alfred
stared after him for a second, and then called, 'Eben, where on
earth ye going?'

Eben whirled around. 'None of your goddamned business,' he
snapped. Then he added, visibly softening, 'And I wouldn't tell
ye that much if ye wan't an old friend.'

This story conforms perfectly to the stereotype of conversa-
tional habits in the country. City people talk a lot, the belief
goes, but rubes are closed-mouthed. They think they've had a
big conversation if one person says he hears Harley's brown cow
is going to calve, and the other answers, 'Ayuh.'

For the first year or two that I lived in the country, I believed firmly in the stereotype. (Even now I wouldn't call it wholly false. There *is* less badinage in the average milking parlor than in the average cocktail lounge.) But I have since come to realize that words can fly as fast in the country as in town. It's just that rural conversation operates under a rather peculiar set of rules. And the rules do impose certain silences.

The first rule is that only the person who's supposed to be talking does. The others keep quiet. For example, say a fellow who might be going to mow your hay comes by on a Saturday afternoon to discuss the terms. His wife and her brother are in the car; they're on their way to go shopping.

In the suburbs where I grew up, there would be some kind of general introduction. 'This is my wife, Alice, and my brother-in-law, Fred.' 'Pleased to meet you, Alice. Hello, Fred.'

There is none of that here. The wife and the brother-in-law sit out in the car, not saying a word. You never even learn their names. Weird, silent, unsocial country people, you think. But it's not that at all. It's just that this is not their deal. If it were, they'd have plenty to say.

I first realized that when I lived for a couple of years in a house that belonged to a rural utility company. This hick utility owned two small reservoirs, and provided water for a New Hampshire town of about seven thousand. The house was right by the lower dam, and normally it was occupied by one of the three employees of the company.

But the guy who'd been living there had just bought a trailer, and the other two weren't interested, so the company rented it to me. It was a terrific deal. I paid a hundred dollars a month rent – this was 1961 – and meanwhile the company paid *me* twenty-five a month to keep people from swimming or fishing in the reservoir. Naturally I interpreted 'people' to mean the general public, but not me, my family, or a few close friends. So for seventy-five dollars a month I had a nice little house plus a private ten-acre lake. Good clean water to swim in, and really great bass fishing.

Every morning the foreman, a man named Asa, would come

by to check the dam and the chlorination unit. He always came in a pickup truck, and he always had his second-in-command with him. (It took two people to deal with the dam gates.) If I happened to be outside when they came, Asa and I would usually have a little chat. I'd tell him how many trespassers I'd driven away; he'd tell me stories about New Hampshire years ago, or funny things that happened while they were fixing pipes in town. The second-in-command never spoke. I didn't even know his name. One of those weird, silent country people.

Then after about six months, Asa was sick one day. But the truck came as usual. The second-in-command was driving, and he had the third employee of the company with him. I was outside when he arrived. As he drove into the barnyard, he stuck his head out the truck window and called cheerily, 'Nice mornin', ain't it? Looks like we'll get spring, after all.' Ten minutes later I knew quite a lot about Denny. We'd swapped a couple of jokes, traded views on baled versus loose hay. He wound up inviting me to come take a look at his farm sometime.

As for the third-in-command, a kid about twenty, he hadn't said a word. I didn't even know his name.

Another rule is connected with rural stoicism. This rule says never admit to caring too much about anything, because if you do, you'll probably lose it. Hence you simply never encounter the phenomenon I used to in the suburbs, where sometimes at a party one of the guests would suddenly look up and say, 'Isn't this *fun!* Aren't we all having a marvelous time!' Except once from a summer person, I have never heard such a remark at a church supper, or at the square dance we have at the end of Old Home Day each summer, or at any Vermont festivity whatsoever. I have seen a good many shining eyes, but heard no gush.

The working of this rule is perhaps clearest among country children. If you invite a city kid to go to the circus, that kid may perfectly well whoop with joy, ask if he can bring a friend, turn cartwheels, if young enough even kiss you. If you invite a country kid, at least in Vermont, the answer is much lower key. 'I don't care,' he or she says.

What that *means* is 'Yes, please, I'd love to go, and you're wonderful to ask me,' but he's not going to spill all that out. You have to get the message from his eyes. You have to look pretty carefully, too, because if he didn't want to go, he might well say the same thing. Only then it would mean something like 'I'm getting a little old for the circus, but if you're determined to take me, I guess I can stand it.'

This trick of speech makes it easy to sort native from non-native children. Just invite all the kids in town to a soda fountain, and ask who wants an ice-cream cone. All the ones who shout 'Me' or 'I want choc'late!' or who groan and say it's too soon after lunch are the children of immigrants from New Jersey. All the ones who say 'I don't care' are natives.

I still haven't mentioned the most important rule. This is the one that's descended from the work ethic. It says that conversation should never be sought for itself, but should just sort of happen. Deliberately to plan some occasion when you do nothing but talk (e.g., a cocktail party) is certainly foolish and probably immoral.

The best way to let it happen is to share a job with someone. *That* you can plan – a quilting bee or a barn raising is just fine – but officially you're there to work on the quilt, or nail rafters; and if there happens to be a steady stream of conversation while you stitch or pound, well, you're just as surprised as everybody else. You came to work.

Hence all my conversations with Asa were just before or just after he checked the dam. When I talk with Rodney Palmer, it's at his garage, and he generally has a wrench in hand. The best conversation I ever had with Wesley LaBombard was while we were planting trees. It lasted seven hours, and ranged from the existence of God to how to raise chickens. Meanwhile, we planted four hundred red pines.

The most remarkable example I know, though, of work freeing a countryman to talk concerns a master mason whom I shall not name. He's a man in his sixties, taciturn even by the standards of rural Vermont. For forty years he has been a silent attender of church suppers (when he goes at all), a silent presence in some summer person's yard, rebuilding a stone wall.

But a couple of years ago a friend of mine who's pretty handy himself got this man to teach him how to build chimneys. In effect, he apprenticed himself. Well! The first couple of days they worked mostly in silence, except for businesslike remarks about hearth laying and lapped courses. Somewhere on the third day they began to trade views about coon hunting. By the end of the week they were into politics.

It was the middle of the second week that the old mason really opened up – never, of course, ceasing to work. At the time he began, they were cutting tiles with a masonry saw, and you are to imagine a noise somewhere between a dentist's drill and a jet takeoff in the background.

It turned out the old man had worked for a couple of years in Boston when he was just out of high school. He had proved very attractive to Boston girls, but in his stiff country way he had repelled their advances. (This, of course, had made him even more attractive to certain ones, who liked challenges.) For forty years he had been wondering whether he had done the right thing to repel those girls, or whether he had been a young idiot. He could remember some of the evenings more or less minute by minute, and he reported every detail. Still, of course, using the masonry saw.

My friend says he talked a blue streak. He would describe a date with one of the Boston girls – it was like hearing a documentary, my friend says – but at the crucial moments he was fairly often sawing a tile. So that what my friend heard went something like this:

'It was about midnight and her folks was all asleep. We were standin' in the hall. I was just going to tell her goodnight, and she says to me' – here he started cutting a tile, and Tom didn't catch another word until the tile fell apart. 'Well, I didn't quite know what to make of that, so I says t' her, "Mary, I don't see as you have any reason to" ' – *neeeeeeyowhh-neeeeeeyowh* – 'and b'gosh if she wasn't trying to drag me' – *neeeeeeyowhh* – 'so, Tom, what would you 'a done if you'd been me?'

Doesn't that sound almost as lively as the average conversation in a bar? Maybe even livelier than some? You know it does. If you want *real* talk, forget the city. Move to the country, and get yourself a job on the road crew (you'll make about $3.25 an hour) or helping some old-timer sharpen axes. During the intervals, when you can hear, you'll learn what country conversation is really like.

Miniature Farming

QUECHEE LAKES IS one of the classier second-home developments in New England. (A Dartmouth student I know
who once worked there tells me that it is inhabited roughly one-
third by rich Irish from Boston, one-third by rich Italians from
New Jersey, and one-third by rich Wasps from all over the
place.) Unlike many second-home developments, Quechee offers more than the standard one-acre building sites – and more
than the usual private golf course, riding stable, tennis courts,
ski slopes, and swimming pool. It also has what it calls farmsteads,
for rich people who would rather have tiny farms than go water-
skiing. This was remarkable foresight on Quechee's part.

A farmstead in Quechee parlance means you get five to ten
acres of land and at least the theoretical right to put in crops.
Not on the back forty, like a Midwestern farmer, but on the
back four, like a New Jersey banker. You can also raise livestock, if you want, and you can have a barn. By no coincidence
at all, every farmstead at Quechee has been sold.

So far none of the forty-odd farmstead owners has put in a
field of durum wheat, nor does any of them raise pigs, or milk
a cow. None, in fact, has done more than keep a couple of
horses and mow a few swaths of hay. But they will, they will.
Miniature farming is the coming sport of the leisure class.

I first became aware of this fact about ten years ago, when
I saw a display of sickle-bar mowers at a county fair. They were

funny little machines with three-foot blades, which hence cut a three-foot swath. You walked behind, holding the handles and breathing the engine fumes. A whole morning's work might produce one mowed acre. The little machines are slow. But when you were done, you had genuinely and indisputably produced hay, which you could rake up with a hayrake, load in your truck with a pitchfork (provided you had a truck), and store in your barn (provided you had a barn). Using one, you felt much superior to your neighbors. There they were, squatting on their riding mowers, fat thighs drooping over the sides, producing nothing but an excessively large lawn. And you, you were farming. I know the feeling well, because at that fair I promptly bought one of the machines. In fact, I still have it, and occasionally use it to trim corners of fields I can't easily get at with my tractor. Before that, for nine years, I used it to mow the whole damn farm ... or at least to do whatever mowing got done.

When I ask myself now why I got the little thing, and waited so long to buy the second-hand tractor I really needed, the answer comes loud and clear. Ten years ago I was still too much of a city person to quite dare buy a tractor. Tractors are big, and have all sorts of mysterious levers. Tractors sometimes rear up, or roll over, and kill farmers. One rolled over last summer and killed a particularly nice seventeen-year-old boy I knew.

By contrast, the little mower is my size – in fact, smaller. If it tips over when I'm mowing a hillside, I can stand it right back up. Often have. If it breaks down, two people can just pick it up, tuck it in the trunk of a car, and take it to be fixed. Try that with an International 504 tractor. In short, with the little mower you feel in complete control from the first minute, even if you know nothing about machines and nothing about hayfields.

And this is the secret of miniature farming. The scale of everything is so small that a completely ignorant city person can buy his five- or ten-acre spread, start fixing it up, and not feel overwhelmed. At the same time, he really is tasting the joy of producing things, for once, and not just being the eternal consumer.

During the last year or two I have met at least a dozen miniature farmers. One is a woman in the suburbs of Boston who keeps seventeen goats – on a three-acre farm. They are, of course, miniature goats from Africa. They're about the size of poodles. It doesn't take a very high fence to keep them in. Should they stampede, there is absolutely no chance of your being knocked down and trampled; if one decides to butt you, it probably tickles. But they yield real goat's milk (a quart at a time), and you could even make tiny *chèvre* cheeses.

Another is a fellow who has succeeded in producing a strain of Belgian draft horses the size of Shetland ponies. A real Belgian weighs pretty close to a ton. Even though the breed is notoriously gentle, a ton of Belgian leaning against a fence (say, a stallion yearning after a mare) doesn't have much trouble pushing it over. Or if a one-ton horse with feet the size of dinner plates happens by pure inadvertence to put his steel-shod hoof down on one of your Adidas, you're very likely to limp for a while. You might even hear a sort of crunching noise. Solution: a matched pair of mini-Belgians hitched to a very small plow, and a very small field of wheat.

Then there is a friend of mine who has just bought one of the new Kubota tractors from Japan. These are real farm tractors done on half-scale. They don't look a bit like garden tractors. A garden tractor has plump little rear wheels with a diamond-pattern tread, and at full throttle could probably be dragged backwards by three miniature goats. A Kubota has proper macho-looking tractor tires with big rubber lugs, front and rear hydraulics, and all the rest. My friend uses his mostly for lumbering. He can only pull rather small trees out of the woods, it's true. But since he does his cutting with a mini-chain-saw, it doesn't really matter. Small logs are easier to split up for firewood, anyway. The important thing is that he's producing his own wood supply with his own equipment.

Another man I know has a bulldozer about the size of a child's kiddie car. Well, it's longer, but not much higher or wider. On the front is a two-foot blade. Then there's a place for him to sit, and steel treads, and a small, rather powerful engine. He loves the thing. It takes him all day, but he can and does grade the driveway that winds up through his mini-apple orchard to his house. It beats golf three ways to Sunday, he says. In fact, it beats sex. (He says.)

Where is all this going to end? Let me report the prophecy of still another friend. This is a New Hampshire man who has lately packed up and moved to Wyoming. The rural New Hampshire town he left is fairly rapidly getting carved up into farmsteads, and junior estates, and just plain building lots, and he happens to like land on a big scale. He's got six hundred acres in Wyoming, and calls himself a smallholder.

Anyhow, here is his picture of rural New England in 1985. There will still be some big dairy farms, he says. Very big ones. But for every big one there will be ten miniature farms, mostly run by former city people. By then there will be a full range of tiny cows (miniature beef cattle already exist), and a full range of tiny farm equipment. What pleases him most to imagine are the tiny hay balers. Having mowed your three acres of hay with your small but genuine tractor, and raked it, and tedded it, you will now bale. The little baler will pop out bales of hay slightly larger than footballs – though, of course, rectangular rather than football-shaped. The whole family will then gather and pitch the bales, one-handed with an overhand throw, up to Father, who will be standing in the hayloft catching them. Farming and sport will have perfectly merged; and touch football in compounds on Cape Cod will have wholly vanished.

Cock Went A-Courting

ONCE I BOUGHT four middle-aged hens. It just so happened that my daughter Amy began begging to keep chickens at the same moment that Aunt Annie Godfrey, from whom we buy eggs, decided to cut her flock down from a hundred hens to seventy-five. She was easily persuaded to put only twenty-one in the freezer, and to sell us the other four.

Aunt Annie's hens were Golden Comets. Golden Comets are a hybrid species, created for life in the hen house. Think of them as large brown birds, broad in the breast and innocent of eye. Very innocent. Few Golden Comets have ever walked by a mother's side, or known a mother's cluck. They are hatched by a brooding machine. Few have scrambled for bugs with other chicks, or pecked a grass salad. Indeed, they are ill-equipped for this, since back in infancy their beaks are automatically trimmed back to stumps. (Beaks are powerful weapons, and just lead to trouble in the crowded conditions of a modern hen house.)

Sadder yet, very few, on reaching adolescence, ever meet a male chicken – or even learn that such creatures exist. Certainly Aunt Annie's knew nothing of sex. They were just four middle-aged virgins, living quietly in her hen house with their virgin sisters. Their total experience of living creatures was limited to other hens and to Aunt Annie. Until I bought them, that is. Then things changed rapidly.

Most of the change was caused by a rooster less than half their size. This rooster – only 'rooster' is too prim a Victorian euphemism for so splendid a bird – this Bantam *cock* had grown up on the farm of friends named Alice and Don Lacey. He was the youngest of seven roosters. The Laceys have a hen house (with attached yard, and real bugs), but he didn't live in it. The senior cock and the fifteen Bantam hens lived there. The six others, the bachelors, lived mostly in the horse barn. All six had grown up on the place – had learned hen talk at their mother's wing, had learned rooster etiquette by watching their father, had grown up dizzy with sex though forever frustrated, because their father could still beat them up. Otherwise they had the run of the place. Sometimes you'd see one playing weathercock on the barn roof; often you'd see a couple roosting in the orchard trees; and oftenest of all you'd encounter a little knot of them having a mock fight with their spurs and their sharp, dangerous beaks.

The day after we bought the hens, the Laceys arrived with the cock in a cage. He was not only the junior-ranking of the six, he had early lost one eye in a fight, and there was absolutely no chance he would inherit the flock of Bantam hens. It appealed to Alice's sense of justice to give him a fresh start in life as sole male around four great buxom brown hens.

When Alice arrived with the Bantam, what he entered as his new home was a little concrete-floored house about eight by ten, with two roosting bars running the length of it and four nests, made of old wooden orange crates, suspended on the wall at one end. At the moment he arrived, in the middle of a Sunday afternoon, his four giant consorts were down on the floor, doing nothing in particular. Alice, Don, my daughter, and I naturally watched through the window to see what would happen.

What happened was that the four hens saw him coming, gave a little squawk of horror, and flew up to one of the roosting bars, where they all perched in a tight huddle at one end. The cock, ignoring this pusillanimous display, strutted to the center of the floor, flapped his wings, lifted his glorious heraldic head, and made a series of crooning noises. These clearly meant something like 'Good afternoon, ladies. [Cocks are extremely courteous, and always have been.] It is my privilege and honor to be your lover from this moment forward. But have no fear. I shan't even come up to the bar until you feel quite secure.'

But, alas, these poor urbanized hens knew nothing of barnyard etiquette. No one had ever taught them what every young pullet should know. They continued to huddle together, abject in terror.

At Alice's suggestion, we decided to give the cock a little assistance. We couldn't let him take the hens out to dinner yet, but we could help him invite them over to his apartment for a snack. To put it more plainly, we went and dug a dozen worms, that gourmet item of bird diet.

When we tossed the worms in, the cock knew right what to do. He ran over to the wriggling pile, mounted guard, and trilled a joyful invitation to his ladies up on the roost. Again, translation is simple: 'A feast, dear ones, a feast!' he caroled. 'And I am saving it all for you. Not one succulent worm will I touch until each of you charming ladies is served.'

Over and over the poor fellow repeated his tender call. But these hens had never heard a cock – knew nothing of the language of love. They knew nothing of worms, either. They stayed put. Finally, he picked up a worm in his beak and held it up toward them. Closely as they were huddled together, they still managed to draw back in horror and disgust. Could that wriggling thing be *food?*

And so we left them.

When my daughter and I went out the next morning to check, three of the hens were still on the perch, right where they had been. But one was down with the cock, and the worms were gone. Curious to see how far her education had proceeded, we went up to the garden, dug a few more worms, and tossed them in.

It had proceeded nicely. While the cock crooned, she seized worms as fast as her stumpy beak would let her. Her relish was so evident that while we watched, a second hen fluttered down and awkwardly grabbed one of the last two.

By afternoon, all four were down, and by the end of a week I had begun to let the little flock out to forage. They quickly learned the joys of the dust bath, and two of the four became expert bug catchers. (This outdoor life had a perceptible effect on their eggs. The yolks turned from a pallid yellow to bright gold, and the flavor went up a full notch.) Though never what you'd call rowdy, all four gradually began leading full and active lives.

But whether because they had encountered the other sex too late in life, or because a mechanical childhood had left them emotionally stunted, or simply because a small one-eyed Bantam rooster is simply not up to Golden Comets, I am sorry to say that our flock of hens lived and died as virgins. They were clearly fond of their little friend, and they would come at his call. But they never permitted him even the slightest liberties. It is possible to be *too* civilized.

Life in the Fishbowl

DID YOU EVER FEEL SORRY for a rock star, doomed always to live in public? If he/she were to slip into the bank to deposit a check for the last three concerts, both the event and the amount would doubtless be in the papers the next day. (That's one reason they have agents.) A simple quarrel with a friend, and it's in six gossip columns. A couple of bad performances, and they wind up on *Boston Magazine*'s turkey list.

At least the rock star – or the football hero or Mrs. Onassis – gets some advantages out of this total publicity. Heads may turn when the famous person walks into the restaurant, and hands may even reach out with pens and idiot demands for autographs. But at the same time, tables turn out to be available, and the service is terrific. There is ego gratification, I'm told, in being in the gossip columns. Some probably don't even mind making turkey lists, provided the accompanying picture is large enough.

In the country, everyone lives like a rock star, except without the advantages. (And, of course, the money and the fame.) Everybody lives, that is, perpetually in public. Heads may not actually *turn* when you enter a restaurant, but you are noticed. There is not a chance in hell that you are going to slip away for a quiet dinner without its going on the local grapevine. It may be a very dull item, merely that you were seen there. Or medium-interest: You were seen with another couple, reliably reported to be your aunt and uncle from Bangor, Maine. They are understood to be staying with you for three days. Or high-interest, and nearly scandal: You were seen having lunch with someone of the opposite sex not your spouse, not a cousin, and in fact not even known to the observer. An item like that is priority traffic, and can make it clear across a rural town in two days.

I suppose people spot their acquaintances in city restaurants, too; and doubtless a pair of prudent adulterers on Gloucester Street would consider having dinner several miles away on Fish Pier. But even if they just went around the corner, recognition would be only a risk. In the country, no matter how far you go, it's a certainty. Unless you drive clear out of the region, of course.

One night last winter, for example, I took my wife to dinner at a newly opened diner seven miles from home. That's what passes for high living with us. (Actually the place is one cut above your standard diner. It has plain New England cooking, but done with skill.) We were late, and when we went in there was no one there but one waitress and one cook, neither from our town. It was calm, quiet, and totally anonymous. Right?

Wrong. Calm and quiet, yes. Anonymous, no. My wife is a jogger, and she has long blond hair. On the basis of these two clues, the waitress came over, handed us the menus, and said pleasantly, 'You must be Mrs. Perrin.' Turns out that when the waitress does her big weekly shop, she takes a road on which my wife jogs. Long ago she had asked a friend on that road who the blond runner was. Naturally the friend knew. The waitress, who wasn't even a waitress then, filed the information away along with the zillion other items that all country people file, certain that some day they'll use it.

That was merely amusing. Sometimes the sense that everyone knows what you're up to can be disconcerting. Take the time I got a check for twelve thousand dollars. A cousin had died, and I was one of the numerous heirs among whom her estate was divided.

The obvious thing to do with a check for twelve thousand dollars is to put it in the bank immediately, before you lose it, or the house burns. I got to the bank within hours. I put it in my account with a certain trepidation, though. The little bank I use is two villages away. Naturally I know all four people who work there, where they live, etc., just as they know these things about me. Now one of the things they would know about was this enormous check.

It just so happens that the year my cousin died was the same year I was grieving about my property taxes. This does not mean that I used to sit and look at the tax bill while tears rolled down my face. It means that I was meeting with the listers and trying to persuade them that my two hundred acres of low-grade farmland was on the grand list at much too high a figure. Under Title 32, Vermont Statutes Annotated, Section 4111, a person has the right to do this on what is called Grievance Day, and the action is generally known as grieving.

I not only know all four people who work at the bank, I like them. I am not in the least suggesting that any of them put the news about that check on the grapevine. There are lots of other ways it could have got there. Or maybe it didn't get there at all, and I simply was feeling paranoid. But it did seem to me, when the listers denied my appeal, that there were little gleams of amusement in their eyes, and that if they hadn't been close-mouthed Vermonters one of them might have said out loud he wan't *too* worried whether I could meet my taxes that year. And I felt a great longing for the blissful anonymity of the city.

I think the extreme case in my life of the fishbowl feeling, though, was the time I went to a psychoanalyst. It wasn't to get my paranoia treated (in fact I think I have only the usual amount). It was to try to help a shaky marriage. I had discovered, seven or eight years later than I should have, that the problems weren't all my wife's fault, after all – that a great many of them were caused by me. I had further discovered that this wasn't something I could change by willpower alone, or even by counseling. Hence the psychoanalyst.

Even in urban centers, going to a doctor to get one's mind treated is a shade less matter-of-fact than going, say, to get some stitches taken when you've cut yourself chainsawing. In the country it is considerably less matter-of-fact. So I was quite willing to keep this little medical adventure to myself.

Fortunately, I was going to a kind of place that's extremely rare in the country. My farm is fourteen miles from a city outpost called the Mary Hitchcock Hospital. There are two great medical centers in northern New England; Hitchcock is one of them. The main building is a small skyscraper. Inside are hundreds of rooms, hundreds of patients, hundreds of doctors. Residents and interns from all over the United States come and go. Very few of them are connected to the rural grapevine.

People with problems like mine go to a separate large building called the Mental Health Center. At least twenty psychiatrists and psychoanalysts have offices there. Probably I would wind up with some doctor from Houston.

I walked rather jauntily into the Center, and found myself in a large waiting room. Six other people were waiting. All strangers. Then I went over to the reception desk – and found myself looking across it at the wife of a man I work with. 'Why, hello, Noel,' she said. 'What brings *you* here?' What did she think it was? Warts?

'Same thing as them,' I mumbled, nodding at the six strangers.

Just then an inner door opened, and a girl named Barbara who lives in a one-room cabin east of our village walked through. She was wearing a white coat. I *had* heard she'd taken a job in town, to pay for building the cabin; now I knew what the job was. She arched an eyebrow in ironic greeting as she passed.

Meanwhile, the wife of my colleague had got my records out, told me it would be a few minutes, and sat me down with the six strangers.

I sat looking at a magazine for perhaps three minutes. Then the analyst I was to have a trial hour with came out to get me. As we walked down the long corridor to his office he chatted a little to put me at my ease. 'You live in Thetford, don't you?' he said. 'My secretary remembers meeting you at a church supper. She's from Union Village.'

If I ever have a guilty secret to hide, I intend to move at once to a city of at least a million.

City Girl and Country Mouse

SARAH WAS COMING for the weekend. My tall, elegant, blond, funny friend, whom I'd first met when she was in college and I just out. That was twenty years ago. Since then, she had been married to a corporate lawyer, and I had drifted from one job to another and finally fetched up as a country teacher and part-time farmer.

Like lots of other old friends in the 1970s, we had gotten together after our respective divorces. It was a joyous reunion – and a prolonged one. All winter and spring I had been spending weekends in her expensive suburb and, to some extent, reliving my own youth in the process. I'd even gone to a country-club dance for the first time since I was twenty-two. But now it was May, and Sarah was going to try a weekend at my place.

My place differed quite a lot from hers. She lived in a two-story house a quarter mile from the beach in one direction, a half mile from fifty posh stores in the other. I lived in an unfinished cabin, twelve feet by sixteen, partway up a Vermont mountain. Terrific views, but no plumbing. No electricity, either, though I *did* have an Aladdin lamp. Aladdins feed on kerosene.

This cabin was my equivalent of the bachelor pad that divorced men in cities move to. (Relatively few bachelors build their own pads, though.) During my marriage I had lived in an old farmhouse in the valley. My ex-wife had it now, which was fair and proper since she also had the kids. I had my mountain, and I loved it.

Sarah knew that she was coming to a primitive spot. She knew that when she flew into our little airport, I would be meeting her in a pickup truck. (In fact, I had often driven the truck down to her suburb, where it was the hit of the country-club dance.) She knew that the cabin's facilities consisted of a spring and an outhouse (well separated) in the woods behind. She even knew that I was off the town road and that we would have to walk the last quarter of a mile.

It therefore surprised me a little that Sarah got off the plane wearing what in good dress shops they call country clothes – meaning lots of camel's hair and tweed – and that she had shoes to match. But she explained that she would have felt foolish flying up in blue jeans and sneakers; she would change when we got to my mountain.

It was a particularly pretty afternoon. Vermont was looking its best. The leaves were half out, and as we walked up the path from where I parked the truck it was like going through green lace. Sarah was enchanted to find the woods dotted with trillium and wild columbine, but a little less enchanted to find the old field in front of the cabin full of ground briers and hardhack. She hadn't exactly expected a *lawn;* she just hadn't realized that someone wearing blue jeans and sneakers without socks would keep getting her ankles scratched.

But she was a good sport. She put on my spare boots (padding them with three pairs of my socks), and we had a long explore on the ridges above the cabin. Along about six o'clock, we hiked back down to the truck and went out to dinner – the kind of country dinner you go to in blue jeans and boots.

Naturally it was dark when we got back to the parking place, a little after ten. I always mean to keep a flashlight in the truck, and I always forget; so we padded up the trail by starlight.

It still gets cold on a Vermont mountain in mid-May, and Sarah was shivering when we reached the dark cabin. Still, she didn't much want to go in. 'How do you know there isn't a

©F. ALLYN MASSEY
'89

bear in there?' she wanted to know. This seemed to me an absurd question. She reminded me that I had told a whole dinner party of people in her suburb, not a month before, that there were bears in Vermont. She further reminded me that that very afternoon when she had looked in vain for a lock on the cabin door, or even a proper latch, I had said scornfully that no one in our town locked his doors.

'There *could* be a bear, and if he wanted to get in, he could just push the door open,' she pointed out with irrefutable logic. About then I realized that to her mind any sensible bear would spend every night of his life indoors if he could, probably would even wish he had a two-story house, like the ones in 'Goldilocks.' I bit back the wisecrack I was about to make – how if there were a bear in this cabin, he certainly had been careful to shut the door after him. I realized she would expect a sensible bear to do that, too.

Instead, I went in and quickly lit two candles, while she shivered just outside. 'No bears!' I called. 'In fact,' I added coaxingly, 'no wildlife at all. Just my nice warm bed.'

She came in, sat on the bed (no chairs, either), and shivered a couple of more times. 'Can we have a fire in that darling little stove?' she asked.

I hadn't had a fire since early April, and meanwhile I had been filling the stove with wood shavings and scraps as I worked to finish the cabin. 'It won't take a second,' I said. I got a kitchen match, touched it to the shavings, and spun the draft full open.

About a second later, Sarah screamed.

She was looking in horror at the stove. After an instant, I saw what she saw. A very small whiskered head was looking out through the stove draft. A field mouse must have moved in to the ready-made bed of shavings I had left; and with his house on fire, he was struggling to get out. But he was so fat (I was careless with crumbs) that he could barely get his body through the little triangular hole.

While we watched, he got one forepaw out, then the other, and then squeezed on out, unsinged. He jumped onto the floor, and Sarah screamed again. Before she would relax, or go to bed, I had to hunt him out of the woodpile and send him packing out the door. I could have wished that some miserable saw-whet owl hadn't picked that moment to hoot a couple of times in the woods behind.

Finally we were in bed, the fire flickering faintly in the draft and a little starlight coming through the windows. We both agreed it was a cozy spot.

When I woke up again it was still dark, and Sarah was urgently shaking me. 'There's a bat in here,' she said. 'It just flew over my face.'

I got up and lit the candles. No sign of a bat. 'I am *not* making it up,' Sarah said. I lit the Aladdin lamp, which with full mantle will equal a hundred-watt light bulb, and we searched the cabin.

A one-room cabin with no curtains and hardly any furniture doesn't afford many hiding places, and finally Sarah agreed that there was no cranny of even bat size left unchecked. She insisted on the reality of the intruder, though, which, since we agreed there was no bat in the cabin now, meant that he must somehow have gotten out. 'Maybe he has his own little door,' she said.

'How come you always say "he"? Maybe it was a she-bat,' I said, still convinced it was really a non-bat. Sarah shook her head, obviously believing that no girl-bat would choose to spend the night alone on a Vermont mountain.

In the morning we had a delicious breakfast, with bacon from a pig I had raised myself. 'You still think I was imagining that bat,' Sarah said, sitting in front of the stove and warming her sweater prior to putting it on.

My smug male smile must have annoyed her, because now, much bolder by daylight, she started a second search for bat hiding places. After a while she found the tag end of a roll of roofing paper under the eaves. Like a roll of paper towels in a suburban kitchen, it had a hollow maybe an inch in diameter in the middle. 'You know perfectly well,' she said, pulling it down triumphantly, 'that a bat could hide in there.' Then she screamed again.

The bat, alarmed at having its house abruptly removed from the eaves, had dropped out the end and was flying around the cabin at high speed.

I can't altogether blame Sarah for feeling that if I had a mouse in there and didn't know it, and a bat in there and didn't know it, I would be quite capable of missing bears, skunks, and rattlesnakes, too. At any rate, we spent Saturday night at a motel in the next town, a rather expensive one, where presumably the tide of rural life never flowed in. And though Sarah and I went on seeing each other for the rest of the summer, and she even came to Vermont several more times, it was perhaps inevitable that for her second husband she picked a city doctor.

Circle of Enemies

I GOT MY FARM at a great bargain: less than 60 percent of the asking price. The reason I got such a good buy was that no one had done any maintenance on it in about ten years. The previous owners had been summer people who gradually ceased coming up to Vermont, because they discovered they preferred Cape Cod. But instead of selling the place, they began renting it out – sometimes just for the summer, sometimes year round. (It was rumored that they kept it in case of war. They felt Vermont would get less radiation than the seacoast.)

Meanwhile, they spent no money on it whatsoever. Oh, a few things got done. A couple of Indiana schoolteachers on sabbatical had the old house for a year, and were inspired to paint most of the wide pine floors a turgid mustard brown. A local deer jacker lived in it for a while, and besides establishing a can dump right outside the kitchen window, he made various changes in the upstairs bathroom. He mounted a heavy iron pipe over the bathtub, supporting each end with a two-by-four nailed to the wall. Then he hung a series of deer over the tub, and later apparently butchered them *in* the tub. This was said to account for the indelible red-brown stains.

But other than a few improvisations like this, no one had lifted a finger on the place. The quarter-mile lead pipe leading up from the house to the spring gradually got more and more leaky. So did the barn roof. Boards on the front porch rotted out. By the time we bought it there had been no tenants in the house for two years, because there had been no water in the house for two years. There was a hole about eight feet by twenty in the barn roof, and an even bigger hole in the floor under it. The beams were horribly flexible; and all that kept the whole structure from playing leaning barn of Pisa was that it is built right onto the house. Little as we paid for the place, there were those, including the first three banks we went to for mortgage money, who thought we had been taken. We heard later that the owner accepted our puny offer only because he knew he had to do *something* that year. He couldn't just have the old barn burned, as people often then did, because the house would have gone, too. So his choices were to sink money into fixing it or taking it down, let it collapse under the next winter's snows, or sell the place.

We took title in late June, which gave us about five months before winter. That same day we started on the repairs. This does not mean I was out there with a backhoe, digging a trench to lay a new pipe to the spring. Or up on the barn roof, either, pulling off leaky metal roofing. At that time, though I'd been around Vermont for several years, I was still essentially a city person and barely capable of fixing a leaky faucet.

The advantage I did enjoy from having been around was that I knew many of the locals. Good, honest craftsmen. What I lacked in skill I hoped to make up for by my knowledge of where to find all the best and most inexpensive barn carpenters, electricians, backhoe operators, and so forth.

Water was the first essential, and we began by getting someone started on the pipeline. I hired a fellow about thirty named Caleb Greenwood. (That's not his real name. None of these names are real. You'll soon see why.) Caleb was a blond, clean-cut young man with a particularly honest, open face. I'd liked him ever since I'd met him at town meeting two years earlier.

The morning he started work, my neighbor on the next place stopped by to watch for a minute. I remarked how lucky I was to have Caleb.

'What you payin' him?' my neighbor asked. I said he had

given me an estimate of 1,800 dollars. That included a quarter mile of new pipe, and new tile at the spring.

'Huh. Caleb always does estimate low. He'll bring ye a bill for twice that.'

'You mean he deliberately underbids?' I asked, appalled. Eighteen hundred dollars represented my income for three months in those days.

My neighbor spat a little tobacco juice. 'I ain't sayin' he's dishonest. Caleb's just a damn fool. And of course he's a drinker, just like his dad. He'll get hung up on every boulder in that field. Wouldn't surprise me if it cost you four thousand.'

This was distressing news, and it made it all the more imperative to economize elsewhere. I decided to ask my neighbor, while he was in this super-frank mood, who could do good cheap work on my barn. He thought a moment. 'If old Levi Parker was still alive, he could jack that thing up,' he said. 'Guess he died afore you come.' This thought seemed to please him.

'Isn't L. F. Parker his son?' I asked, proud of my knowledge of local relationships. 'The one they call Sonny? What about him?'

'*Him?* Oh, he does good enough work. Got good men workin' for him, too. But ever since he started bidding on jobs down to the college, he's got pretty damn expensive.'

'Oh.'

We watched Caleb in silence for a moment. He had his backhoe hung up on a huge boulder. For a man working on my time, he seemed deplorably unconcerned.

'So who would you suggest?' I finally prompted.

'There's people in town could *do* it,' he said. 'Earl LaJoy ain't bad, if he'd ever finish a job.' He thought even longer. 'I believe if it was me, I'd go over to Starkfield and get the Mayhew brothers.'

Starkfield is the next town to ours. It feels farther away than the four miles it is, because to get there you have to cross the river on a bridge, and when you have crossed you are in New Hampshire. In some ways Starkfield is foreign territory.

Still, I had friends there. Good friends. The kind you can

ask for the lowdown. The next day on my way home from work I swung over to check out the Mayhew brothers. Henceforth I intended to get at least two opinions on any potential workman.

My best friend in Starkfield was a fellow in his late twenties, a logger. We talked chainsaws a little while; I had just bought my first one. 'What do you think of the Mayhews?' I asked presently. 'Would you trust them with your barn?'

'I wouldn't trust them with my chicken coop,' Lee answered instantly. 'Two most pigheaded men in town. You could be standing right there telling them what you wanted done, and if they happened to feel like doing the opposite, they'd nail right on past you.'

Lee gave me a curious look. 'What are you thinking about the Mayhews for, anyway, when you've got Sonny Parker not two miles from where you live?'

'Too expensive.'

'*Sonny?* Why, he was the low bidder by six hundred dollars when they fixed up the church steeple. He's the kind of guy who would figure out a way to sell you a hundred-dollar bill for ninety-nine–fifty. Just like old Levi was.'

'That's not what I heard.'

'Who'd you hear it from?' Lee asked. I explained about my neighbor. Lee burst into laughter. 'Pay no attention. He and Sonny are second cousins. My ma told me they had a fight over a girl when they were both at the Academy, and they're mad yet. Thirty years later.'

A notion was beginning to dawn in my mind. I immediately put it to the test. 'Do you know Caleb Greenwood?' I asked.

'Since we were kids.'

'You got any opinion on his work with a backhoe?'

'I had him dig the trench when I put in my well,' Lee said simply. 'He's the best. You can ask anyone.'

A few minutes later I drove on home. Caleb had left, but when he came the next morning at 7:30, I wandered out and talked with him a few minutes. He had dislodged the big boulder, pulled out at least a dozen others, and was already about six hundred feet up the trench.

'I want to ask you something,' I said after a while. 'You aren't any relation to – ?' I gestured down toward my neighbor's house.

'Nope.' Then he grinned. 'Why? He tell you something bad about me? Thought he might. The first year I was in business, I did a job for his brother Pete. Cost eighty dollars more than I told Pete it would. We hit ledge. Pete didn't want to pay, and I guess we had words.'

He smiled even more broadly. 'I could tell you a few things about him, too. Like the time he had two does hanging in the bathtub in your house. Fellow living here then did a regular business butchering out of season.'

Ten minutes later we were still talking. On my time, as I thought (though it later turned out Caleb charged the flat 1,800 dollars, and wasn't even keeping track of time), but I also thought it was well worth it. I had steered the conversation to the Mayhews, who Caleb assured me were among the best builders in the whole region. Better than Sonny Parker and Earl LaJoy, for example.

I mentioned Lee's warning. Caleb laughed out loud.

'Why, hell,' he said, 'they're his wife's uncles. Course he wouldn't say anything about *that*. It's a funny town, Starkfield. More goddamned feuds going on. New Hampshire's like that.'

So it is. Vermont is also like that. From what I've heard, Maine is, too. Country people may be more charitable in other parts of the United States, but in New England there's a simple rule to follow, if you don't want to conclude that every neighbor you have is a scoundrel. Make inquiries about them one town away.

A Passable Farmer

BLACKS QUIT PASSING for white, I'm told, about a generation ago. Who would want to be mistaken for a honkie? But city people still like to pass for countrymen. The object is to deceive other city people. Both temptation and opportunity are particularly strong if you lead a double life anyway – are urban in the winter and rural in the summer, or an office worker during the week and a farmer on weekends.

I come in this latter category. During the week I wear a coat and tie, and am a professor. Students have been known to call me 'sir.' Weekends I wear sweaty overalls, and shovel manure. Students, seeing me at a distance as they drive past my place, have been known to shout, 'Hey, Mac! Which way to Union Village?' But that's no test. The real thrill is to have a close-up encounter . . . and to emerge from it with disguise intact.

Such encounters happen fairly often. A typical incident goes like this. Some friend in town has a clump of birches in his backyard, which get sick and die. (Birches do this all the time.) Knowing I have a chainsaw and ropes and a truck, he suggests I come take the trees down, and we'll divide up the wood, and then I'll stay for a drink and dinner.

So I show up about four in the afternoon in my battered old truck, wearing sweaty overalls, and drop the birches. But because yards are very small in town, there is no way not to drop the two that lean west onto the neighbor's property. The neighbor is an old lady. We knock on her door, and get her rather reluctant permission. She then hovers at the kitchen window, watching, so that she can catch me in the act if I hit any of her shrubs. I don't. Luck is with me, and I am able to drop both birches right between her smokebush and the forsythia.

Now I come over onto her property to cut the wood up. At this instant she shoots out the kitchen door. She addresses her neighbor, not me. 'Peter, tell your man not to start that saw yet. I want to talk to him.'

My heart suddenly plummets. Was there some *little* bush I didn't see? A bunch of perennials? Neither. She is pleased with my work. In fact, I am about to be offered a job in the way that middle-class people offer them to laborers. 'How much are you charging Mr. Bien to take those birches down?' she asks, looking me firmly in the eye, and sounding very cultured. For a minute I feel as if I'm back in the third grade. 'If you're reasonable, I may have some work I want you to do.'

The first time I was ever offered a job this way, I got into a dither. I didn't really want the job (I had classes to teach the next day, and midterms coming up), but I didn't want to blow my cover, either. I was reduced to mumbling. But by now I'm long practiced.

'Sorry, ma'am,' I say. 'This ain't my reg'lar line of work. I'm just helping Mr. Bien out. But I can give you the name of a good tree man, if you want.' She does, and I do. We part happily, the mistress and the handyman.

The supreme encounter of my life so far happened a few years ago. I was a newly promoted associate professor at the time, and also newly launched in the selling of maple syrup and firewood from my farm. A young assistant professor had ordered a cord of wood from me, and I arrived with it one Saturday afternoon in the fall. His in-laws happened to be on a visit at the time.

When I rolled in with the wood, Tom promptly came out to help me unload and stack it. He was closely followed by his father-in-law.

Tom's father-in-law was not one of your average, everyday
fathers-in-law. Tom had been a Rhodes scholar, and while at
Oxford he had met and married a Chinese girl from a very
wealthy family in Malaysia. The Wangs, as I'll call them, were
principally into tin mines and rubber plantations. They were
as at home in London and Paris as in Kuala Lumpur. They
shared to the full the old upper-class Chinese prejudice against
manual labor. When Dr. Wang followed his son-in-law into the
yard that bright New Hampshire morning, he was wearing a
cutaway coat, striped trousers, and a pair of pearl-gray gloves.
His mind was not in the least on me; it was on the indignity of
seeing his son-in-law unload maple logs from an old Chevrolet
truck.

'Tawm,' he said in his really quite elegant accent. 'Tawm,
have you nothing better to do with your time? It's this fellow's
own fault he didn't bring a helper.'

Tom unloaded another armful of logs, and said nothing.

'You're dressed disgracefully,' Dr. Wang continued, thoroughly enjoying himself. 'What if one of your students were
to see you?'

Tom loaded up again, still silent. Dr. Wang strolled about the
yard, swinging by my truck to remark (to Tom), 'That lorry
is filthy. Do you suppose he *ever* washes it?'

It took us about half an hour to stack the cord; and while
Dr. Wang didn't stay with us the entire time, he came out at
intervals to reproach Tom, and even once to comment unfavor-
ably on my appearance. (I didn't wear overalls in those days,
but I did have barn paint on my shirt, and I was unshaven.)
This was fascinating. I had read that in Victorian England people could talk in front of the servants as if the servants didn't
exist, but I had never experienced it before, especially from the
servant's point of view.

When we finished, I started to get quietly in my truck and
be off. But Tom had other plans. Taking me by the arm, he
steered me firmly over to his father-in-law.

'Dr. Wang,' he said in his most formal, scholarly tones, 'I

should like to introduce Professor Perrin, my superior in the English department.'

This coolie was a mandarin? Dr. Wang heard the words, but his mind couldn't fully accept them. A lifetime of urbanity enabled him to offer me his hand – but whether he wondered at the last moment if Tom was playing an obscene joke on him, or whether it was pure reflex, he snatched it back before I could shake it. By sheer will he forced it out again. As I reached for it, again he jerked it back. On the third attempt, we shook hands. By now he was so nearly flustered that to regain his composure – or maybe just do the right mandarin thing – he invited me to have lunch with him at the Hanover Inn on Monday. I went, too. Considered wearing work clothes, went instead in the one three-piece suit I own. We never once alluded, either of us, to wood or trucks or paint-stained shirts.

The one time I failed completely to pass was with a college undergraduate. Not one from my own college, but a fellow who was just hitchhiking through New Hampshire. I was on my way back from helping a friend to butcher two pigs when I stopped to pick him up.

Approximately two minutes after he got in the truck he turned and said casually, 'What college do you teach at, sir?' I almost ran off the road.

'Dartmouth,' I blurted. 'But how could you tell?'

'Easy. You talk like a professor, and you just sort of act like a professor, and then there's that.' He pointed to the top of the dashboard, where I had carelessly left a copy of Faulkner's *Light in August*, which I was then teaching in English 78.

Since then I have attempted to fool only persons aged about twenty-three and up. College students I just wave to from the barn.

One Picture Is Worth Seven Cows

FIRST PERSON RURAL was, if possible, an even more rustic book than this one. The essays in it have minimal relevance to regular American life. One talks about making butter from raw milk; another gives many useful tips about fence posts. Nevertheless, through some miracle my publisher managed to interest both *Time* and *Newsweek* in reviewing the book.

As a result of those reviews, I have gotten two sharp insights: one into the rivalry between *Time* and *Newsweek*, and one into urban life. It's even more different from rural life than I had remembered. More intense, sure. Faster, naturally. But especially it's more concerned with what from a country point of view might seem minor matters ... such as what I am about to describe. The amount of time and effort that urbanites will put into almost anything is downright awesome.

The story begins on a hot Wednesday afternoon, two days after *Time*'s review came out. Before I tell it, I have to explain one thing about that review. It had a picture with it, as book reviews in *Time* usually do – a picture acquired in what I think of as a 'normal' way. That is, *Time* got it from my publisher, who had used it on the dust jacket of the book. Godine had gotten it from me, and I in turn had gotten it from Richard Brown, the talented Vermont photographer who took it. *He* had retrieved it from the files of *Vermont Life* magazine, where it originally appeared. What it shows is me out in the pasture mending fence, closely watched by seven cows. It's a good picture, especially of the cows. Brown had a credit line in all three places.

Now back to the story, and that hot Wednesday afternoon. I was not mending fence; I was sitting in my office at Dartmouth College, grading papers. The phone rang.

'Mr. Perrin? This is Lisbet Nilson at *Newsweek*. We're going to review your book.' I liked the voice immediately, and would have even if she had said they were going to shred my book and use it for sheep bedding. 'But there's a problem,' she went on. 'We need a picture of you. We can't possibly use that thing that was in *Time*.'

What they wanted to do, she said, was to get a new picture taken. They would engage a photographer and set everything up, provided I was willing to cooperate. Was I?

Was I! The thing almost any writer likes best is getting reviewed. The thing he likes better than best is getting reviewed in magazines with very large circulations.

'Well, then,' she concluded, 'if you'll give me Richard Brown's phone number, I'll call him and get things started.'

But I couldn't do that. I didn't have his phone number at the office. I have it written in the back of the phone book at home. So I offered to copy it on a postcard that night, and mail it to her first thing in the morning.

Ms. Nilson burst into merry laughter. 'Come on, Mr. Perrin, you've worked in New York, *you* know how we do things. I need that number in the next twenty minutes. We want to get the picture taken tomorrow. Tell me what town he lives in, and I'll get the number from Information.'

But I couldn't do that, either, because at the time I didn't know what town Richard lived in. I only knew it was well north of my part of Vermont.

'Never mind,' she said. 'There are two photographers in New Hampshire we sometimes use. I'll get one of them, and call you back. You can be available either morning or afternoon tomorrow, right?' Right.

But when she called back, there was still a problem. One of their two New Hampshire photographers had gone to work for the Associated Press, and the other (I was proud of him) was in the middle of roofing his barn. He feared rain on Friday, and refused to take Thursday off to go picture taking. 'I guess it's back to Richard Brown,' she said. 'What time are you going home?'

'Be there about quarter of five.'

'Good. I'll call you at ten of five, and get his number.'

She called on the dot, and I had his number ready. Meanwhile, she had had another idea. 'Since you know Mr. Brown, why don't you give him a call first and prepare him? Tell him I'll be calling in about fifteen minutes.'

By now I was almost as involved in setting this up as Lisbet was (we had become Lisbet and Noel at some point in this, our third long-distance conversation of the day), and I was glad to do that. But though I let the phone ring eighteen times, there was no answer. Since Richard has a wife and small children, I concluded they must all be away on a trip. It was right on five o'clock, the very moment when small children are in the house, getting baths and supper and reading.

So I called another photographer I know, just to see if she'd be available, assuming she was acceptable to *Newsweek*. When I got no answer, I called her ex-husband to see if he knew where she was. When I couldn't get him, I called the editor of *Vermont Life* to ask for the names of more photographers. He and I are old friends.

'Why do you need others?' he asked. 'Richard's around. I saw him a couple of days ago. He's probably just out on his tractor. Call at dark, and I bet you'll get him.' But he gave me some more names, just in case.

We had hardly hung up when the phone rang. It was Lisbet, cheerful but frustrated. I told her what I had done, and offered to call Richard at sundown and make the arrangements.

'This is a formal assignment for *Newsweek*, and I really should talk to him myself,' Lisbet said. Then she hesitated. 'But you're pretty informal up there, aren't you? You go down to the general store, and you make business deals by shaking hands over the cracker barrel, right?'

I assured her this happened all the time. It's true, too, all but a couple of details. We don't *have* a cracker barrel in the general store, and hardly anyone in town shakes hands on a deal. Word of mouth is enough. But deals certainly do get made in the store. Last time I was in there, I sold a fellow a gallon of maple syrup. Once a friend of mine bought four goats while he was picking up his mail.

'O.K.,' said Lisbet. 'Tell Brown that *Newsweek* wants him for half a day tomorrow. Our half-day rate is a hundred and twenty-five dollars.' Wow! 'Tell him we want between fifty and a hundred black-and-white shots. We want him to get you doing as many different things as possible on your farm ... except,' she added casually, 'we don't need any cows. And tell him to phone me as soon as he's done, so we can arrange for an air courier to pick up the film.'

At this point I must have whistled, or possibly said something like 'Gosh all hemlock!' Twenty years in Vermont have got me into such habits. Lisbet laughed again. 'That's not as grand as it sounds,' she said. 'We don't have a fleet of jets. It's just that all over America there are these little men who like nothing better than to drive to your front door, pick up a package, and take it to the nearest airport. There *is* an airport somewhere near you, isn't there?'

I would have loved to have been able to say it closed five years ago – but, alas, it's actually expanding. Three flights a day to New York, I told Lisbet, and a fourth threatened. 'Good,' she said. 'We're set. I'll call you in the morning to confirm.'

We were set. Richard came down the next day, with two cameras, and he took 108 pictures. 'This is an awfully high-energy way to get one shot to go with a book review,' he remarked at about picture 57 – but he kept shooting. Lisbet meanwhile found an air courier, and at seven p.m. on Thursday the film was winging its way to New York.

Ten days later, the review appeared in *Newsweek*. Instead of a picture of me with seven cows, there was a picture of me with one sheep. It's a good picture, especially of the sheep. But I can't help computing that by the time you add up the twelve phone calls, the fee, the mileage from where Richard lives to where I live and back, the air courier's charge, the cost of getting the film from La Guardia into *Newsweek*, my time, Lisbet's time, the time of whoever developed 108 pictures, and the time of whoever else spread them out and chose one to print – it would all add up to enough to buy seven more cows. And I can't help thinking it would be a better use of the money.

A Fool's Guide to Splitting Wood

ONE OF THE GREAT American dreams is the foolproof machine. By definition, it requires no skill or experience to operate – any fool can do it. Most of us own a lot of them. An automatic toaster would be a fair example. If you can push a handle down, you can operate a toaster.

The average lawnmower is an even better example. Lawnmowers are so foolproof that though they all come with a little manual (instructions about winter storage, warnings about flying stones, etc.), it's a rare buyer who actually reads it. He doesn't have to, and he knows it. He just takes his new machine home and starts mowing. Two years later, when the damn thing won't start after thirty pulls, *then* he may try to remember where the manual is. May even find it, still in its clear plastic case.

Cars are a better example still. Most of them have a series of little lights – idiot lights, I'm told they're called. Do you need to add oil? A little light will tell you. Time to have the emission controls checked? On goes another little light.

Or consider the matter of shifting gears. How many of us decide with our own brains when to do this? About seven percent. The other ninety-three percent have paid extra to get a shift that makes the decisions all by itself.* It may use more gas,

---

* These figures apply only to buyers of American cars. I can't find comparable statistics for those who buy imports. But I would guess that half or more pick a standard shift.

but it sure does save thinking. The fool at the wheel needs merely to keep his or her foot on the accelerator, and the car rumbles from one gear to another as it sees fit.

Foolproofery is by no means limited to machinery. It can be found even on the commercial fringe of the fine arts. Any hobby store sells a dozen kinds of kits designed so that a person with no talent and no experience can nevertheless paint a passable landscape. Lines on the canvas mark where the sky is to be blue, where the fluffy clouds go, and so on. (Signs in the studio say when to applaud.) The kits may not produce great art, but then, you can paint a complete picture the very first day. An apprentice of Titian's might have had to wait five years before he got a whole canvas of his own.

Until very recently, the process of getting up firewood was immune to all this. It openly required skill. Even the arrival of technology did not foolproof it. Using an ax may have required *more* skill than using a chainsaw, but both require it. To see the new owner of a chainsaw timidly trying his or her first cut, holding the thing like it might be a present from the PLO, and to see the same person's easy dexterity a year later is a real reassurance of the value of experience.

As for splitting, that takes the most skill of all (except maybe for making a tree fall where you want it to). You've got to know where to place the wedges, how to handle a maul, how to give your ax a little twist just as it hits the wood. Even stacking the wood you've cut and split takes a touch of skill. It is rare indeed for someone to produce a neat pile, end-stacked and stable, the first time they try.

With the new boom in wood heating, however, foolproof devices and machines are beginning to flood the market. You can buy a little machine that will sharpen your chainsaw for you (it says), even though you don't know how to sharpen a chainsaw. Or even a small chainsaw that will, after a fashion, sharpen itself. Just as you can have a fire that practically starts itself. There are at least four kinds of foolproof kindling currently on the market. No need to worry about getting the paper crumpled just right, the smaller wood laid just so. If you can light a match, you can start the fire.

But since splitting is the trickiest part, no-skill splitters are what have really poured onto the market. They come in many varieties, and at many prices. The most expensive rely on brute force to replace judgment. In traditional splitting, you become an expert on wood grain – you know just where the easy cleavage is, just how near you can get to a knot or a branch stub and still make the log split. With a 900-dollar hydraulic splitter, you just ram it through any old way. A good-sized engine and a can of gasoline are the substitutes for judgment.

This isn't to say that hydraulic splitters don't have their genuine uses. For really big logs they are a godsend. I confess to owning one that mounts on my tractor, and to using it on just about any log larger than two feet in diameter, and on *all* yellow birch. There's a danger, of course, that one will wind up using it even on a piece of straight-grained oak that one could almost tap apart with a kitchen knife – just as you sometimes see construction workers who have become so dependent on their giant machines that they'll spend five minutes maneuvering a bucket loader up to a thirty-pound rock, even though it would be much quicker just to bend down and pick it up.

Lower down in the price range there are the screw-type splitters that you mount on a car wheel, and which produce the messiest-looking split wood known to man. Then there are special axes that have a sort of metal truss built onto the head, so that you don't have to learn the knack of the little twist. Finally, and newest of all, there's a foolproof wedge.

As anyone who has ever split wood knows, regular wedges are flat-sided. There are two kinds. One kind is simply a wedge-shaped piece of steel, and if you are splitting a very large, very knotty piece of wood, you might have to drive in two or three of them with a sledgehammer before it goes. The other kind is designed to be mounted on a handle, and when it is, you call it a splitting maul. That's what most of us use most of the time. And most of us wind up fairly proud of our ability to judge just

where to come down on the log, and of our good eye in being able to come down on that exact spot again, if the log doesn't split on the first blow.

The new foolproof wedges eliminate all that. They are round, not flat-sided, and look like large metal ice-cream cones. Instead of *deciding* where to place one, you simply tap it into the center of the log. Then you drive it in hard with your sledge or maul. Being round, it doesn't exert pressure just in two directions, but all around the circumference of the log. When the pressure gets great enough, the log will split along its natural lines of least resistance. It doesn't matter a bit that the person doing the splitting has no idea where those lines are. The wedge finds them for you. If you're new to the wood business, this is an appealing notion.

The name of the new wedges makes them even more appealing. They're called Wood Grenades – in fact, that's a trademark of the large and reputable company that makes them. (Omark also makes the majority of chainsaw chains.) What that name suggests to me is that after a couple of blows the log will virtually explode into a nice pile of firewood.

When Wood Grenades appeared on the market last year, I was doing all right with my maul for most logs, and with the tractor splitter for especially big, mean ones. But being curious – and having that vision of a log exploding into four or five stove-sized pieces – I promptly bought one to try it. This was the original model, a stubby steel thing, painted a soft gold, and thus quite easy to lose on the forest floor. (What with dead leaves, pine needles, etc., the ground in the woods is usually painted a soft gold itself.)

The first time I tried it, I tapped it into the center of a log – and it promptly fell out. I tapped it back in. Then I began to whang it with a sledgehammer. No explosion. In fact, nothing happened at all, except that it gradually moved deeper into the wood, and I gradually got out of breath. Finally, after what seemed like twenty blows, the log lackadaisically fell apart.

The next log split the same slow way. When the third and

fourth also did, I concluded there must be some trick I hadn't
learned yet. So I wrote to Omark asking for advice. They re-
plied that you just start the Grenade in the center of the log –
and they also sent me a present: a new, improved model. This is
a long, slender cone, made out of what seems to be magnesium.
It's silver colored, light to handle, and easy to find on the ground.

One morning recently I took the two Wood Grenades and
my regular splitting maul, and set out to do a systematic test.
First I went to the north end of my woodlot, where I have been
cutting down a group of bull maples. I cut three logs, nine inches
in diameter and twenty inches long, from the same upper stem.
It was a slightly crooked stem with curly grain – about par for a
red maple that has grown up in what was once a pasture – and
therefore sure to be hard splitting.

To be fair, I took the biggest of the three logs for my maul.
I looked for a natural splitting line, and went at it. The log
shivered neatly into two on the fifth blow. About par for that
kind of wood.

Then I set up the next-smaller log, and tapped in the old-
model steel Grenade. That made the log top-heavy, and it
promptly fell over. I set it back up, and propped it with the
two pieces I had just split. Then I whanged the Grenade eleven
times, after which the second log shivered neatly in two. A little
more than twice as much work.

Finally, I set up the third and smallest log, and tried the magnesium Grenade. It really is an improvement. The log split in
only six blows – and furthermore it split into three pieces. Not
bad. But not great, either. The diameter was decreasing, and
the splitting was getting easier. When I cut a fourth piece off
that same stem, the maul took it in three swift cracks.

So it went with all the tests. I next tried a whole bunch of
seven-inch-diameter logs from another maple. One easy blow
with the maul split each one. The magnesium Grenade required
an average of five blows per log, and the steel averaged seven.
On the butt log of a smaller maple, thirteen inches in diameter,
I had to hit the steel Grenade thirty-seven times before the log

reluctantly came in two. When I tried some white pine, to make sure my results weren't special to maple, a similar pattern instantly appeared. Clear pieces of pine eight inches in diameter I could always split with the maul in one blow. Knotty pieces took two or three blows. With the magnesium Grenade, I had to strike an average of four times on clear pieces, seven on the knotty ones. The steel Grenade did about the same.

Here, it seems to me, is a clear victory for skill over salesmanship. The Wood Grenades really are foolproof (if you can find the center of a log, you can use a Grenade), and they really do work. They just don't work nearly so well as the tools they are intended to replace. Which figures. After all, if they're exerting pressure all around the circumference of a log, it stands to reason that they're not exerting very much in any one direction. Whereas flat wedges concentrate all their power in just two directions.

Despite their slowness, Wood Grenades and the like may still appeal to novice woodcutters. I'll even concede that such things have their uses. But it's satisfying to know that modern technology doesn't *always* win – that a man (or woman) with an old-fashioned maul and the skill to use it can turn out firewood faster than with any other hand tool.

Garden Animals

W H O   C A N   D I S P U T E   I T ? The Rototiller is to the garden as the washer and drier are to the laundry room. Before washers and driers got invented, and began to contribute their marvelous speed and high electricity consumption to American life, the housewife slaved over a hot tub. Maybe she then enjoyed putting everything out on the line with clothespins. Maybe she loved the smell of those sunshiny sheets. But it sure was slow, compared with popping everything in a drier. On rainy days, not even slow. Impossible.

Before Rototillers came along, with their marvelous speed and high gasoline consumption, husband or wife slaved in the vegetable garden, right? Dug the whole damn thing over with a spade. Weeded it with a hoe, the way Thoreau did those two and a half acres of beans at Walden. He used to hoe every day from five a.m. until noon, and then knock off and go swimming. That's seven straight hours of bean hoeing, and yet Thoreau was regarded by the serious gardeners of Concord as a loafer. The serious gardeners were right. Despite all that work, he never got all his rows tended even once. He should have hoed afternoons, too.

As gasoline gives out, we are going back to *that?* Forget it. There's more to life than raising vegetables. While there's a supermarket left with a package of frozen Fordhook lima beans, while there's even a can of starchy dull-green peas to be bought, most of us will choose to buy it rather than to become again the Man (or Woman) with the Hoe.

Happily, these are not the only choices. Modern Americans have almost entirely forgotten it, but before there were garden machines there were garden animals. There can be again. When gasoline is two dollars a gallon, or when gasoline is unobtainable except with a ration ticket, I am pretty sure that not just the horse but the cow, pig, goat, and sheep will once again figure in our horticulture. Not in flower beds (they'd eat the perennials), any more than Rototillers do now. That aspect of gardening has remained manual right along, which is why the size of flower beds has shrunk in direct proportion to the availability of hired gardeners. But in vegetable gardens, even in some suburban ones, I think one day we will again hear oinks and moos and baas.

Thoreau in 1845 knew all this perfectly well. What we tend to remember from *Walden* is the solitary figure of the philosopher, hoeing or meditating, but in actual fact he used garden animals. He paid seven dollars and fifty cents to have his bean field plowed and furrowed by a team of horses. Once when he got tired of the five-a.m.-to-noon routine, he paid a boy with a one-horse cultivator to come for three hours and weed between the rows. That cost a mere dollar. He *could* have had horse-cultivating right along, if he hadn't been curious to see how little money he could spend, and how much of the work he could do unaided.

I began to use garden animals about fifteen years ago. I had no prophetic vision of the coming energy shortage, I was just feeling experimental. I had a forty-foot-by-forty-foot vegetable garden, and because of the deer I had it quite tightly fenced. When I bought two piglets to raise, it seemed to me it would be a neat idea to turn them into the garden after I had harvested. They could clean up the old cornstalks and salvage any potatoes I had missed. Turn this debris into top-quality fertilizer with no effort on my part. And finally plow the garden for next spring.

That particular idea was not a success. They cleaned up the

cornstalks, all right, and ate the potatoes. They even made the fertilizer. But pigs are much more fastidious animals than I then realized, and they weren't about to spread the manure evenly, as I had imagined. Instead they converted one corner of the garden into a bathroom facility, so that in cold November I was out there trying to rake pig droppings around with frozen fingers. (Well, actually with a *rake*, which I held in frozen fingers.)

Much worse, though they did plow the garden, they had not that interest in a smooth graded surface that nearly all gardeners have. They were more like two excited archaeologists on a dig. They left the surface full of holes and excavations, many of them big enough for two pigs to lie comfortably in. I had a stiff job later with Rototiller, rake, and hoe, restoring order to that field of devastation.

But that was an apprentice effort, and apprentice efforts are probably supposed to fail. Later efforts have been much more successful. In the fall of 1978, for example, I put a couple of half-grown lambs in the garden for three days in September, and again for three days in late October. The first time, they ate the cornstalks, etc. (No potato digging. Any I missed just quietly rotted.) The second time, they neatly trimmed the annual ryegrass I use as a cover crop. Both times they did a light but well-distributed fertilizing job. Furthermore, they later contributed four legs of lamb and a great many chops to the dinner table, which is more than any Rototiller has ever done. For that matter, I've never had a Rototiller's hide tanned to use as a throw rug.

Last fall I did better yet. I was able to borrow a friend's flock of fourteen sheep for a week, and each night I used the garden as their sheepfold. The result was a fairly thorough fertilizing job, and a surface that will require only the quickest of Rototillings next spring. Also a week's illusion of being a real farmer.

But the greatest triumph with garden animals I know of was won by a neighbor of mine, who keeps milk cows. He has three, and supplies a good many people in town with unpasteurized milk.

Garden Animals

It being cold in Vermont in the winter, once a year the cows have to endure five straight months of being cooped up in the barn. But they do get to go out every day for a constitutional while my neighbor does his cleaning and puts down fresh sawdust. On a sunny, mild day, they may get to be out in the barnyard for five or six hours. Cows being what they are, the barnyard naturally gets quite heavily manured, and it becomes practically sodden with urine.

Come spring, Floyd fences off the sunniest quarter of the barnyard, and there he plants a part of his garden. No black plastic for him, to keep the weeds out. The cows have packed the ground so hard that passing weed seeds just bounce off.

In this tough surface, Floyd makes just enough holes to plant his tomatoes and cucumbers and peppers. He doesn't plant many. Last summer, for example, he had four tomato plants. From those four plants he supplied his family and his daughter's family – and gave a couple of bushels away. It was the same story with peppers and cucumbers. I didn't know plants *could* grow like that. They say that in Iowa you can hear the corn growing. It seemed to me that I could see Floyd's tomatoes grow. I don't say they swelled as fast as a child blows up a balloon, but they did visibly change size in a single day. Plants may think they like bone meal and homemade compost, but what really excites them is to live where cows have been. If you planted a geranium in Floyd's barnyard, I expect you'd have to cut it with an ax.

Not everyone has, or wants to have, milk cows. Still fewer would fancy a barnyard garden. But almost anyone could use a pair of lambs as gardening tools. One pair of lambs could probably handle a dozen gardens each fall – could be a cooperative venture of a whole neighborhood. Or if owned by a single proprietor, could be quite profitably rented out by the night. Goats would work, too, provided the fencing was tight.

For that matter, almost anyone could use piglets. What I didn't know fifteen years ago was that there's an easy solution to the excavation problem. You just buy an old smoothing harrow. (It looks like the headboard of an iron bedstead, and because there were vast numbers made in this country in the nineteenth century, none of which are of the faintest use in agribusiness, they cost very little.) Then you get a neighbor with a horse. It will take the horse about ten minutes to pull the smoothing harrow around your garden. You wind up with a surface you could play billiards on. If you're really lucky, the horse may even leave you a present of two or three pounds of choice fertilizer. You'll know right where he left it, next year. It's the place where one cornstalk is a foot taller than all the rest.

Rototillers aren't going to vanish, any more than washers and driers are. At least I hope they're not. But even if they do, I think human beings are still going to find gardening easy, and a pleasure. With the help of a few friends.

The Rural Immigration Law

EACH MAN KILLS the thing he loves, Oscar Wilde wrote
in a poem that later became a popular song. As a general statement, this won't do. Lincoln didn't kill the Union; lots of men
don't kill their wives; so far from killing the ERA, Betty Friedan
and Kate Millett have worked hard to keep it alive.

But practically all tourists and most people who move to the
country do kill the thing they love. They don't mean to – they
may not even realize they have done it – but they still kill it.

The tourist does it simply by being a tourist. What he loves
is foreignness, difference, the exotic. So he goes in search of it
– and, of course, brings himself along. The next thing you know
there's a Holiday Inn in Munich.

The case with people who move to the country is more complicated. What they bring along is a series of unconscious as-
sumptions. It might be better for rural America if they brought
a few sticks of dynamite, or a can of arsenic.

Take a typical example. Mr. and Mrs. Nice are Bostonians.
They live a couple of miles off Route 128 in a four-bedroom
house. He's a partner in an ad agency; she has considerable
talent as an artist. For some years they've had a second home in
northern New Hampshire. The kids love it up there in Grafton
County.

For some years, too, both Nices have been feeling they'd like
to simplify their lives. They look with increasing envy on their

New Hampshire neighbors, who never face a morning traffic jam, or an evening one, either; who don't have a long drive to the country on Friday night and a long drive back on Sunday; who aren't cramped into a suburban lot; who live in harmony with the natural rhythm of the year; who think the rat race is probably some kind of minor event at a county fair.

One Thursday evening Don Nice says to Sue that he's been talking to the other partners, and they've agreed there's no reason he can't do some of his work at home. If he's in the office Wednesday and Thursday every week, why the rest of the time he can stay in touch by telephone. Sue, who has been trapped all year as a Brownie Scout leader and who has recently had the aerial snapped off her car in Boston, is delighted. She reflects happily that in their little mountain village you don't even need to lock your house, and there *is* no Brownie troop. 'You're wonderful,' she tells Don.

So the move occurs. In most ways Don and Sue are very happy. They raise practically all their own vegetables the first year; Sue takes up cross-country skiing; Don personally splits some of the wood they burn in their new wood stove.

But there are some problems. The first one Sue is conscious of is the school. It's just not very good. It's clear to Sue almost immediately that the town desperately needs a new school building – and also modern playground equipment, new school buses, more and better art instruction at the high school, a different principal. Don is as upset as Sue when they discover that only about forty percent of the kids who graduate from that high school go on to any form of college. The rest do native things, like becoming farmers and mechanics, and joining the Air Force. An appalling number of the girls marry within twelve months after graduation. How are Jeanie and Don, Jr., going to get into good colleges from this school?

Pretty soon Sue and Don join an informal group of new-comers in town who are working to upgrade education. All they want for starters is the new building (2.8 million dollars) and a majority of their kind on the school board.

As for Don, though he really enjoys splitting the wood – in fact, next year he's planning to get a chainsaw and start cutting a few trees of his own – he also does like to play golf. There's no course within twenty miles. Some of the nice people he's met in the education lobby feel just as he does. They begin to discuss the possibility of a nine-hole course. The old native who owns the land they have in mind seems to be keeping only four or five cows on it, anyway. Besides, taxes are going up and the old fellow is going to have to sell, sooner or later. (Which is too bad, of course. Don and Sue both admire the local farmers, and they're sincerely sorry whenever one has to quit.)

Over the next several years, Don and Sue get more and more adjusted to rural living – and they also gradually discover more things that need changing. For example, the area needs a good French restaurant. And it needs a *much* better airport. At present there are only two flights a day to Boston, and because of the lack of sophisticated equipment, even they are quite often canceled. If Don wants to be really sure of getting down for an important meeting, he has to drive. Sue would be glad of more organized activities for the kids. There's even talk of starting a Brownie troop.

In short, if enough upper-middle-class people move to a rural town, they are naturally going to turn it into a suburb of the nearest city. For one generation it will be a very nice and a very rustic suburb, with real farms dotted around it, and real natives speaking their minds at town meeting. Then as the local people are gradually taxed out of existence (or at least out of town), one more piece of rural America has died.

This is happening to large parts of New England at the moment. The solution, as I see it, is a good, tough immigration law. It wouldn't actually keep Don and Sue out, it would just require them to learn rural values before they were allowed to stay. When they moved to the country, they would be issued visas good for one year. At the end of that year, they would have to appear before a local board composed entirely of native farmers, loggers, and road-crew men. They would then present evidence of having acclimated. For example, they could show proof of having taken complete care of two farm animals of at least pig size, or of one cow, for at least nine months. Complete care would be rigorously interpreted. Even one weekend of paying someone to feed the pigs or milk the cow would disqualify them. (An occasional trade, on the other hand, would be acceptable. Don and Sue could take care of a neighbor's stock one weekend, and thus earn the right to be away the next, while he looked after theirs.)

Such a rule might work a hardship on elderly people moving to the country – say, if Sue's parents decided to come up from Baltimore. For them there would be an appropriate modification. The old couple wouldn't have to learn how to handle cattle at sixty-eight and sixty-three. They wouldn't even have to get up on the roof of their house, like natives, and shovel snow or replace missing shingles. But they would have to do undelegated work. For example, if they both worked in the kitchen at all church suppers during the first year, personally cooking beans and making the red-flannel hash, that might earn them a visa renewal. A cash donation would get them nowhere.

What if the board didn't pass you? I'm kindhearted. I wouldn't say you had to clear out immediately. It's just that your taxes would automatically double. They'd stay double until you passed your preliminary test.

And if you did pass? Why then you'd get a five-year visa under the same conditions. By then a seasoned pig raiser, woodlot manager, or church-supper worker, you would appear before the board a second time. If the board approved, you would then be an Accepted Resident – and, incidentally, perfectly free to spend all your time playing golf, trying to turn rural schools into suburban schools, etc., etc. But I'm guesssing that very few immigrants would. It's so much more interesting to keep pigs.

What about all the second-home owners who aren't residents anyway? That's easy. Double all their taxes right now.

The Year We *Really* Heated with Wood

To boast in 1978 that you have a wood stove is about like telling people proudly that you own a TV set, or that your kitchen has a sink. By the latest estimates, more than half of all rural New Englanders run a wood stove these days. In places such as northern Michigan the proportion may be even higher.

But to *have* a wood stove and to depend on wood for your principal heat are two very different things, as my family and I discovered last winter.

We are old hands with wood stoves. For the last fifteen years we've been living on a Vermont farm. The house had an oil furnace when we bought it – and the farm had a big woodlot. No oil wells, however. So fourteen and a half years ago we set up a couple of stoves: one in the kitchen and one in the living room. We've used them, too. Saved a significant fraction of our heating bill, and all that. Never had any problems. A few years ago we even added a third stove – a nice little Jøtul in the guest room upstairs, which has always been cold. But we ran it only when we had guests.

Then came the well-known rise in the price of fuel oil. By the spring of 1977 the stuff was selling around here for fifty-one cents a gallon, which at the time seemed high. What had been half a game for fourteen years suddenly became serious business.

By then I was an experienced woodcutter. Experienced enough to know that my woodlot could yield ten times what I had been cutting, and actually benefit from the process. Why not step up production? So in the spring of 1977 we decided to switch from System A, an oil furnace supplemented by wood stoves, to System B, wood stoves supplemented by an oil furnace. This is the story of what happened. Or part of the story, anyway. I haven't been able to get in everything, like my wife's learning to play the piano twenty minutes at a time, and then dashing into the kitchen to wash a few dishes, because none of our stoves really gets to the room where she keeps her piano. But the main elements are here.

March 7, 1977. Today we paid 526 dollars for a new stove. If we're really going to heat with wood, we need a really powerful stove. It's got to handle four rooms downstairs and four more upstairs – everything, in fact, but the kitchen and the guest bedroom. So we've taken out our hundred-year-old cast-iron parlor stove and replaced it with a brand-new Defiant. As a fringe benefit, we will gain some space. One of the Defiant's advantages is that you can mount a heat shield behind it, and then put it practically up against a wall.

March 8. I took the day off from work and spent it entirely on the stove. If it's to go where my wife wants it, we need a new stove hole on the left side of the chimney. Our neighbor Lee Ilsley came and cut a perfect round seven-inch hole through the chimney bricks with hammer and chisel. Then I helped him install the thimble. The rest of the day I devoted to buying stovepipe, setting it up, building a new and larger woodbox, and so on. Tonight it all looks worth it. The Defiant is tucked away beside the chimney, looking very handsome. The back is only five inches from the brick house wall.

The old stove used up about a third of the room.

April 8. Maple-sugaring ended two days ago. Starting today, I am spending my free time cutting next winter's wood. I already have about four cords I cut last fall – but with System B I figure I will need at least twice that much. It is already late to be cutting wood that will be dry enough.

The Year We Really Heated with Wood

April 9. Today is Saturday, and I spent the whole day in the woods. It would make sense to cut all the trees I'm going to, right now, so they could start drying. But psychologically that doesn't work for me. It's too much like an assembly line. I prefer to take one tree at a time, fell it, buck it up, and do all the splitting, before I move on to another. Today I did about a tree and a half. Both were red maples eighteen inches in diameter. A tree this size yields something over two-thirds of a cord.

April 23. I'm past the eight-cord mark, and still cutting. My wife has started coming out with me, to help with the splitting. She learns fast.

May 2. We've decided to cheat a little on the wood. Counting last fall's, we have nearly ten cords of long wood for the Defiant cut, split, and stacked. That was fun.

But I'm getting tired of cutting very short pieces for the two little stoves: the Ulefos in the kitchen and the Jøtul in the upstairs wing. So we have ordered a truckload of scrap from Malmquist's mill, four miles away. It's what is left over after they make blanks for chair legs, and it's mostly pieces of rock maple and yellow birch six to twelve inches long. You get about a cord and a third for forty dollars.

May 28. We've had a dry spell, when I could get my truck into the woods. Most of next winter's firewood is now stored in the barn, ready for use.

It's been a problem spreading all that weight around. Our barn is built right onto the house, and it has a cellar, just like the house. Earlier owners kept their cattle down there. I don't want to keep our wood down there, because it would mean lugging every armload up the stone cattle ramp next winter. But I'm scared to keep too much in any one place on the main barn floor, for fear of breaking the beams. Result: I have five different piles of about half a cord each, plus two cords stacked on the ramp itself. Another cord and a half is outside, stacked against the west wall of the barn.

There's a connecting shed between the house and the barn (the cellar goes under that, too), and that's where we used to keep practically all of our wood. This year it just has the short wood for the two little stoves. About three cords of it, counting the load we bought. The maple from Malmquist's is awfully heavy. I worry a little about having stacked it six feet high.

May 31. We haven't lit a fire even once this week. Heating season is over. I cleaned the stoves, and spread the ashes in the back pasture. Lilacs are at their height, and apple blossoms almost over. We've got peas up six inches.

September 12. I haven't thought much about heating systems for the last three and a half months. Been too busy gardening and raising sheep. Last night's frost and this morning's kitchen fire reminded me, though. It's time for the next project, which is to insulate the cellar. People have warned me that if we don't run the furnace regularly, our cellar will freeze. But I have a solution. Most of the cold gets in where the house cellar meets the barn cellar. I am going to build an extra wall eighteen inches outside the existing wall, and fill the space with sawdust. The old-timers used to keep ice all through the summer by burying it in sawdust; I reckon I can keep icy air out the same way.

September 17. The wall is built. It took a full pickup-load of sawdust to fill the space – and it must be one of the least expensive insulating jobs on record. A hundred and twenty cubic feet of good hardwood sawdust cost me six dollars.

I may be imagining it, but the shed floor seems to have developed a slight slant.

October 1. Cold, steady rain for the last two days. We've had two stoves going, and the house is beautifully warm. Who needs a furnace?

October 4. The rain has continued, and we are using wood at a good clip. It is already clear I don't have enough stored. No problem. I've got plenty more cut and stacked in the woods. All I need is a few dry days to take my truck out and get it.

October 5. Perfect sunny day after a sharp frost. I went out at dawn, while the ground was still hard, and brought in two more cords. It's stacked on the front porch, leaving just enough space for the door to open freely.

I am not imagining the slant in the shed floor.

The Year We Really Heated with Wood

October 6. After work, I went down to the barn cellar with a flashlight. All three beams under the shed are badly bent. The central one has cracked, and is on the verge of breaking. I borrowed two jack posts from my neighbor Barbara Duncan, and spent the evening trying to jack the center beam back up. No luck. The woodpile up above is just too heavy. But at least I don't think the floor will sag any more. I'll worry in the spring about how to straighten the beams.

November 24. Snow today. We just smile and stoke our stoves. We have yet to use the furnace this winter.

December 8. I didn't use screws when I mounted the Defiant's stovepipe, and a couple of sections are beginning to come apart. We are not eager to have the house burn down. Annemarie let the fire go out this morning, so that this evening I could take the pipe down and reassemble it with screws.

Since it was five below zero when she got up, this naturally meant starting the furnace. I wasn't altogether sorry – even though I had hoped to go until Christmas. Our water pipes run under the kitchen, just inside the new sawdust wall. Somehow the cold is getting through. Last week I took a thermometer down there. This morning it registered thirty-six degrees. A little hot air in the furnace pipes will be a good thing.

December 10. We've been back on stoves for two days, and it is now thirty-three degrees inside the sawdust wall. I consulted my friend Tom Pinder, who is clever about such things. With his help, I've vented the clothes drier directly into the cellar. (More accurately, he did it, while I passed him tools.) Come spring, we'll shift the vent back outside.

December 11. The coldest day so far this winter. Minus twelve. The pipes to one bathroom were frozen. The water pump, miraculously, was not, though the cellar thermometer read twenty-eight degrees this morning. I took down a bucket of coals from the stove.

December 12. Twenty-four hours of running all three stoves at top heat have failed to melt the frozen pipes. The problem is that the warm air from the stoves can't get at the pipes. They're in the walls – right next to the air ducts from the furnace. No one was thinking about heating with wood when this house was plumbed.

December 13. Shut down the Defiant again, and let the furnace run all day. Even though the temperature never rose above six degrees, we succeeded in thawing the pipes out. Starting today, I am leaving the furnace turned on. The plan is to keep the thermostat set low (the markings only go down to fifty-two degrees, but you can actually set the dial at about fifty) – and then count on the furnace to come on for a couple of hours late each night, just enough to keep the cellar warm and the pipes unfrozen.

January 25, 1978. The system is working perfectly. It doesn't even take much oil. We had our second delivery of the winter today. The tank got topped off in September with 28 gallons, and today it took 140 gallons. And we are halfway through the winter! Other winters, we have used five or six hundred gallons by now, even with the old parlor stove going most of the time. (And if we had ever tried a completely stoveless winter, this big brick house would have drunk 900 gallons by now. I know, because once we rented the house for a year and our tenants never lit a match. They got through almost 1,800 gallons in what was a fairly mild winter.)

February 4. The system *was* working perfectly. Yesterday the temperature dropped to fourteen below. Today it's twenty below, and windy. Even though I left the thermostat at fifty-eight instead of the usual fifty last night, we have no water this morning. Two buckets of coals in the cellar before I went to work brought the water back by noon – but I don't want to spend my life providing hibachi service for water pipes. Before next winter I shall either put a little stove down cellar or figure out a way to insulate the rest of the cellar walls, or maybe both. This morning it was twenty-six degrees next to the sawdust wall. And thirty-seven at the other end of the cellar, where I keep the wine. California and France make poor training for a Vermont winter. I hope the wine wasn't too upset.

February 16. Another bitter day. We have now used all the wood on the front porch, all the wood on the stone ramp, and three of the other five piles. There's still some stacked outside along the barn wall, which I never had room to bring in last fall – but it is currently buried under six feet of snow, piled up when the barnyard was plowed.

I see two choices. I can dig it out, or I can go to the woods and cut dead elms. Otherwise, we seem certain to run out of wood before spring.

February 25. I chose to cut dead elms. This was a sunny Saturday, delightful to be out, and I spent nearly all day cutting on a low hillside, and then riding the wood out on a toboggan. Got a two-week supply (at February-March burning rates).

March 15. Today we had our third and final oil delivery: 169.6 gallons. Then we turned the furnace off until next winter. I'm no longer worried about pipes – we're already into mud season, and there wasn't even a frost last night. And I'm not worried about wood, either. The dead elm didn't quite last two weeks – but the powerful March sun has already melted the snow away from the barn wall where I had wood stored outside, and I can get at the top rows easily.

We used 337.6 gallons of oil, at a total cost of 178 dollars, 13 cents. This is lower than our oil bill ten years ago. In the winter of 1967–68, despite help from two stoves, we used 1,317 gallons of oil at 16.6 cents a gallon, and it cost us 218 dollars, 34 cents. Who says there's inflation? The *country* may have inflation, but this farm is enjoying deflation.

It's true that I've got to fix the shed floor, insulate the cellar, think about getting another stove, worry about the piano room, plan better storage facilities in the barn, and fetch home ten cords of wood – but, then, I enjoy doing most of these things. Keeps my weight down, and it's a hell of a lot more interesting than jogging.

As for the wood itself, it was cut and split last fall and winter. In fact, while I was at it, I cut twenty cords instead of ten. What we don't use, I shall sell. After deducting expenses in woodcutting, and the cost of whatever oil we buy, next winter I expect the process of heating our house to produce a cash profit. We may just blow it on a trip to Saudi Arabia.

POSTSCRIPT, 1980. We have now been through three winters on System B. Only it's not System B anymore, it's System B-plus. Practice does help.

Oil consumption has continued to decline. The second winter it dropped more than a hundred gallons, down to 204. Last winter, with heroic effort, we pushed it on down to 137. This, I suspect, is about as low as it's going to get – at least if we want to continue using the plumbing.

As to cost, our private deflation continued for a second year. In 1978–79 our total oil bill was 120 dollars, 49 cents. That is surely the lowest oil bill the house has ever had, even though it got its oil furnace back in the bargain days of 1950. It may even be lower than the coal bills the previous owners were paying in the 1940s. And since I sold 600 dollars' worth of wood, we did get our cash profit.

But last winter our slowly descending use curve met OPEC in round three, and was soundly defeated. For that one solitary delivery of 137 gallons, an unfeeling oil company charged us 139 dollars, 74 cents. One more rise of that magnitude and we will probably shift to System C, a wood furnace. (If we do, we'll put hot-water pipes through it, and so get free hot water six months a year.)

Meanwhile, we have been busy learning new tricks about managing with wood stoves. Most important, we have learned how to keep a fire going pretty well continuously. Back in the old days, I would have to split ten or fifteen boxes of kindling every fall – and the first person up every morning normally had to build a fresh fire in both stoves. Now we use maybe two boxes a winter. Every member of the family knows how to cram the Defiant so full at bedtime that there will still be plenty of coals in the morning. And we all know what proportion of the ashes to take out and just how to rake the coals so that starting the day's fire amounts to no more than putting in fresh wood. (You have to put it in right, of course – and not all at once. They don't call it *building* a fire for nothing.)

Furthermore, we run only one stove now, except on the very coldest days. The little kitchen wood stove is still there, and it's very handy for burning milk cartons and the boxes pizza comes in. Between that stove and the pigs, we don't have much garbage in the winter. But as for keeping the kitchen warm, we do that primarily with a tiny fan. It's four inches square, and it's mounted in the top of the doorway leading into the kitchen. Except when the temperature is ten or twenty below zero, it blows in enough heat from the Defiant to keep the kitchen comfortable. I no longer cut much short wood.

At the cost of shutting off one bathroom from mid-December to early March, we have completely avoided frozen pipes upstairs. The cellar is a little harder; and in really cold weather I am still running the hibachi service. That's another inducement to move to a wood furnace.

But even the cellar doesn't cool off as readily as it used to, because we did indeed do more insulating. In the fall of 1978 I repointed the cellar walls, caulked around the windows, and stuffed fiberglass in wherever any would fit. Then, since there was nothing left to do inside, we started on the outside. Late that fall, copying something we'd heard people used to do a hundred years ago, we banked the house with spruce branches. You make a sort of festoon of them, all around the foundation. It looks pretty, like a giant Christmas wreath laid clear around the house.

But spruce branches turn out to be only so-so insulation. So last winter we tried a different system, employing slightly more modern rural technology. I had a bunch of hay bales that had got rained on (which makes them unappetizing to cows – and less nutritious as well), and I gave the house a necklace of hay. Hay bales do a superior job. Cellar temperatures averaged a couple of degrees higher.

But since I hope not to get any hay rained on this year, and I'm certainly not going to use good cattle hay, worth a dollar-fifty a bale, I have an even more advanced plan for next winter. All the leaves from the ten or so maples in the yard I intend to put into those big green plastic bags you see being carted away in suburbs where it's no longer legal to burn leaves. Only instead of carting mine away, I shall stack them like pillows all around the foundations. A big maple drops a lot of leaves. On the back side of the house, which is also the north, I may have leaf pillows three deep and three high. Right up to the windows, in fact.

People who notice the rapid rate at which our Defiant burns wood sometimes wonder if we won't burn ourselves right out of trees in a few years. The answer is no. Unless I get tired of cutting, we can go on this way forever. Our farm includes just about a hundred acres of woodlot. In a cold climate like Vermont's, an acre of trees will add about half a cord of new growth per year. So our annual production is 50 cords – 900 cords of new wood in the eighteen years we have owned the place.

Some of that growth, of course, is in pines and hemlocks, which we would not use for firewood. Quite a lot is in good, straight yellow birch and ash and sugar maple, trees that it would be criminal to buck up for firewood. But at least a third of it is in trees that ought to come down anyway – red maples that are busy rotting at the core, crooked oaks, black cherry that's getting shaded out and dying. I could cut fifteen or twenty cords a year indefinitely, and just be improving a still-increasing timber stand.

In actual fact, I cut twenty-six cords last year – sold seventeen and kept nine. (Grossed 1,124 dollars, 75 cents; netted plane fare for one to Saudi Arabia.) This year I may cut thirty cords. That still won't be borrowing on the future. It will merely be catching up with the past. Of the 900 cords that have grown while we've been here, about 650 are still out there on the stump. A couple of hundred, at least, are in the form of trees that ought to be thinned out. Even though I never want to have a forest that is wholly practical – with no hollow trees for the raccoons and no 300-year-old low-branched maple stubbornly clinging to life and not growing an inch – I still have a mighty backlog to draw on. In fact, from the point of view of getting this farm in shape, fuel oil at one dollar, two cents a gallon is about the best thing that could have happened.

Pig Tales

1. THE PIG AS ARTIST

Pigs get a bad press. Pigs are regarded as selfish and greedy – as living garbage pails. Pigs are the villains in George Orwell's *Animal Farm*. Pigs have little mean eyes.

There is truth in this account – not that it's entirely the fault of the pigs. For perhaps five thousand generations pigs have been deliberately bred to be gluttonous. Out of each litter men have picked the piglets that were least solicitous of their brothers and sisters when nursing; have set aside the shoats that hogged the trough most and were most thoroughly selfish; have butchered the adult pigs that showed any signs of moderation, and kept the ones that had the most ravenous appetites and gained weight the fastest. This was their breeding stock. Do the same thing with human beings for five thousand generations, and it would be interesting to see what kind of people resulted.

The marvel is that pigs have been able to keep so many interesting character traits despite fifty centuries of such single-minded breeding. For example, I once had two pigs who were artists. At least, I think they were. At a minimum, they were ingenious carpenters.

These two I had bought as piglets, and they were my first livestock, my first year living on a farm. I treated them handsomely. They had a fenced pen forty feet square (it was going to be our garden the next year), and they had a little house. The house was an old wooden shipping crate I had found in the barn, to which I had added a peaked, wood-shingled roof. There was no need to give their house a roof of shining cedar shingles – I had just happened to find about a third of a square of unused shingles when I was cleaning the barn, and it amused me to make an elaborate house for the piglets.

While they were little, they paid the roof no attention at all – didn't seem to notice it. They slept in the house, close together in the hay, and otherwise they were out digging in their yard. But when they got to be about three months old, and were already good-sized shoats, they began to help each other climb up on the roof of the house. As far as I could tell, they did this for the same reason that Sir Edmund Hillary climbed Everest. The challenge interested them, and they liked the view. I minded slightly, because they tracked mud all over the clean shingles, but mostly I enjoyed seeing them up there, staring calmly into the distance.

Then one early-fall evening, when the pigs were about five months old, I came home and found the roof gone. Well, not the roof, but every single shingle, and most of the nails. The pigs had not only pulled them off, they had split them into pieces averaging four to five inches wide, and they had made a cedar shelf all along one side of their pen. A cedar shelf forty feet long. It was made of dirt raised about four inches above the ground level, and topped with a continuous row of split shingles. It must have taken them most of the day, especially since they had neatly removed the nails.

Clearly a cedar shelf had nothing to do with food, nor could it have been part of a plan to escape. By raising the ground level four inches on that side, they were in fact making escape harder, since pigs escape by burrowing.

I see only three possibilities. One is that the little sow (I had a barrow and a sow) wanted to improve the housekeeping arrangements, and got her brother to help her put up the shelf for storage. But as they never kept anything on it, I consider

that unlikely. The second is that it had religious significance. It *was* the eastern side of the pen they chose, and the autumn sun rose right over that shelf. But as they never performed any ritual whatsoever, I discount that possibility, too. I think they were making a work of art.

The shelf lasted five days, and then one afternoon I came home to find it completely gone – the dirt as well as the shingles. The shingles were in a pile, ready for some further use later; the dirt had been merged back into the general garden. But, then, much twentieth-cenutry art *is* ephemeral, by design. I think Bingo and Bacon weren't interested in a work for the ages, but in a Happening.

This was their masterpiece, but not their only work of art. They never did anything more with the shingles. (I eventually used them for kindling.) But in the two months more that they lived, they three times filled their troughs with mud. Each time, they got the mud exactly even with the top of the trough, and smoothed it until there was almost a patina. I can't say much for the color values, but the texture was stunning. Judging by the last trough especially, earth art is really more a pig form than a human one.

11. FREUDIAN PIGS

My next pair of pigs were also a brother and sister. They had no artistic leanings, but one of them at least had considerable psychological complexity. That year I was getting most of my pig food from a big commercial bakery. The bakery had a thrift shop, where you could buy store returns for half price. What didn't sell there was available to pig owners for two cents a pound. Before you could buy, you had to sign a pledge that you wouldn't feed any of it to human beings. (I broke the pledge almost immediately. My second or third trip, instead of the usual pallid bread, I got about fifty pounds of English muffins, and a hundred pounds of little pies and cakelets. I tried everything. Stale but edible.)

These two pigs had been named by my six-year-old daughter,

and they were called simply Sow and Boar (pronounced boor). Boor was greedy even for a pig, and he normally allowed his sister no more than a third of the food. When I came back from the bakery with pies or muffins, he did his level best to keep her from getting anything at all.

What I should have done, of course, was to make another trough and put it on the far side of the pen. Boor would have tried hard to keep her away from both troughs, but since they would have been forty feet apart, I don't think he could have succeeded.

What I actually did was to play policeman. On pie-and-cake days, I would fill their trough and then stand there with a good-sized stick as the two pigs came hurtling in. Both would get their heads deep in the pastry. As soon as he was swallowing regularly, Boor would turn and give Sow a battering-ram blow with his head, and she would squeal and back up about three feet. Then keeping one small, mean eye on her, to make sure she didn't try to sneak back, he would set about eating the whole vast troughful himself.

At this point I would interfere. Since I am one of those who think that policemen should give warnings before they start making arrests, I would give Boor a light tap. That meant: Move over, boy, and let your sister have some. He would respond by speeding up his already rapid feeding pace.

After the warning, the summons. My next step was to give him a good whack in the ribs. He would then back up just long enough for Sow to race in for a bite – and then, looking like a pink animated tank, he would come thundering back, wham Sow out of the way with one mighty blow, and plunge his snout in. At this point he got two whacks. That caused him to retreat about ten feet, where he would stand with blazing eyes, cursing shrilly in his throat. As far as I could tell, the curses were aimed equally at Sow and me, as joint conspirators in the plot to do him out of his dinner.

After a minute he would control himself, though, and it was at this point that he became a Freudian pig. He had the sense to sublimate. First he would trot across the pen and take a good drink of water. Then he would lean against one of the fence posts, close his eyes, and begin swaying back and forth in such a way as to give himself a lovely scratch. His eyes weren't *really* closed, of course, because if I now turned to tiptoe away, he was back across the pen at rocket speed, and once again battering Sow with his head.

But if I stayed, he would finish his rub, have another leisurely drink of water, and then, setting that powerful head of his like a dozer blade, he would move deliberately into the center of the pen and start excavating. He put the full force of a strong personality into these excavations. I have known him to get so involved that I could actually leave, and be as much as thirty yards away, before he noticed and sped back to the trough. His craters and trenches were not art, they were only displacement, but they worked. Boar could deal creatively with the frustration of his deepest interests, which is something I can seldom manage myself.

III. THE DARING YOUNG PIG

One thinks of pigs, or at least *I* think of pigs, as essentially earthbound creatures. They have massive bodies on small legs. They spend a lot of time lying down. Their escape technique is invariably the tunnel. Once even half grown, they are terrified of heights. I have caught an escaped shoat of under two hundred pounds, because he had reached a retaining wall less than thirty inches high and stood trembling at the edge, afraid that if he went over he might break a leg.

It was for this reason that I was so long in figuring out how one of my next pair of pigs kept getting out.

At that time I was experimenting with a portable pigpen. The theory was that I would keep a pair of young pigs in it all summer, moving the pen about to wherever I wanted brier bushes or burdocks or milkweed dug up. Then in the fall, when we had harvested the big fenced garden, we would pop the pigs in there. They would plow and fertilize it for next year.

The theory was not a sound one. For one thing, there is not enough level land in Vermont for a portable pigpen to be tight at the bottom. For another, a pig-plowed garden looks more like a battlefield where both sides had heavy artillery than it does like a smooth planting surface. The one really successful period out of that whole summer and fall was the first three days after the pigs had entered the garden. Then, appearing and reappearing among the cornstalks and the tall weeds, they looked like a painting by Henri Rousseau.

My story, though, takes place the second week in May. I had just built the portable pigpen, and just put the piglets in it. They were exactly a month old, pink with black spots, slightly larger than footballs. The pen was one day old, made of rough-cut hemlock boards spaced two inches apart. I made it eight by five, and two and a half feet high. As good as a football field to pigs that size.

A couple of hours after I had put the pigs in, one of them was out and trotting on her little hooves over to my wife's flower beds. She wasn't too hard to catch. A little milk in a dish, and she came right over, docile as a kitten. I took a careful look around the bottom of the pen, saw there was a tiny dip in the land, decided she must have squeezed out there. I moved the pen to one of the few absolutely level spots we have. Twenty minutes later the same little pig was out again. Absolutely no sign of digging. There was no way she could slip through two-inch gaps between boards. Logic said she must therefore have gone over the top. Could she be climbing, using the gaps as footholds? It didn't seem likely. But she clearly *was* getting out, so I raised the sides one more board, this time not leaving a space. The pen was now three feet high – the same height as a fence for adult cattle. The top foot was solid smooth board.

It amazes me now that I could have thought I had the problem solved, but I did think it. I calmly went in to lunch, sure that the piglets were now secure.

Before lunch was on the table, the little sow was back in the flowers. Being quite full of milk by now, she was harder to catch. In fact, it took two people. This time, though quite hungry myself, I decided to linger near the pen and see what her escape route was. I got behind a tree and waited.

In about two minutes she came sailing over the top of the pen, made a four-point landing, and trotted briskly off toward the peonies. She had jumped three times her own height.

I had to put a chicken-wire ceiling on the pen before she would stay in, and she had to make twenty or thirty jumps before she would believe the wire would hold her.

What if we had spent five thousand generations breeding pigs to jump, instead of to stuff themselves and lie down? By now the most sluggish hog among them would be able to enter barns by the second-story windows, and farming would be an even more picturesque business than it already is.

IV. PROTECTOR OF PIGS

Mickey Jamieson and I were on a pig-buying trip. We had a pile of burlap sacks in the back of the truck, some baler twine to tie them with, and a little money. Our destination was Mr. Harrington's barn in Sharon, Vermont, reputed to contain more pigs than any other structure within fifty miles. Neither of us had ever been in it, though we had both driven by in the spring, and been awed by the sight of thirty or forty brood sows out in the fields grazing.

Crossing Sharon Ridge on the way, we had stopped to visit with a farmer Mickey knew. Before we left, Mickey had parted with two ten-dollar bills and acquired two very small piglets. This was why one of the sacks in back was tightly tied, and had some tendency to move under its own power.

We pulled up in front of Harrington's barn, and turned off the engine. We did not get out. The reason was that an absolutely giant Saint Bernard had appeared from inside the barn. He came bounding up to the truck, put his front paws on the rear bumper (the truck sagged perceptibly), and shoved his head in the back. He seemed to be looking for something. When we tried opening a door, he raised his head and growled deep in his throat.

After a minute Mr. Harrington emerged from the barn. He, too, came over and looked in the back of the truck. Then he smiled. 'He's worried you're hurting them piglets,' he said. 'He can smell 'em, and he can hear 'em squeaking. It upsets him. If he was sure it was something you're doing, you'd *never* get out of that truck.'

It turned out that the dog was one Mr. Harrington looked after for some summer people. 'But he don't know that. He thinks he belongs here. And he thinks God put him on earth to look after pigs.'

Inside, the barn was a pig buyer's dream. There was a seven-hundred-pound boar taking a nap on a pile of hay. Ranks of sows in stalls. In a big space at one end, something like fifty piglets flashing around like a school of minnows. Many of them the black-spotted kind that Mickey and I both favored.

The dog paced with us as we walked up and down the barn with Mr. Harrington. As we walked, Mr. Harrington told us stories about different ways a Saint Bernard eases life for pigs. Some of the stories could only be repeated in a bar toward the end of the evening (or in a pig barn at any time). These were the ones about the big dog's failure to understand mating behavior in the pig world. A young sow of three hundred pounds is sometimes coy and willing simultaneously. When that happened at Harrington's, the Saint Bernard took her squeals for help as completely serious. He would interpose his massive body between the loving couple. He was even prepared to bite where it hurt most. More than once a fully aroused seven-hundred-pound boar had found himself trotting meekly back to his end of the barn, pretending that all he wanted was a quiet rest.

Some of the stories were about tourists. Harrington got a lot. Not regular tourists, but country people from twenty or thirty miles away who just wanted to see that many pigs in one place. He ran a kind of all-pig zoo. In winter, when farmers have the most free time, he averaged a set of visitors a day.

One set consisted of a young couple and their four-year-old

son. The mother and the boy were nice enough, Harrington said, but the father was what he called ugly. The boy kept asking questions, and the father kept telling him to shut up. Soon the father announced that one more question and the kid would be damn sorry he'd asked it. There was silence. But after a few minutes the little boy turned and asked Mr. Harrington if he could get in and play with the piglets.

The father must have been waiting for this, because his hand moved back instantly, ready to cuff. The blow never struck, however. The dog had been pacing behind, and when the hand swung back, he caught it firmly and apparently rather painfully in his teeth. The whole party stopped. The father looked back cautiously over his shoulder. 'What do I do now?' he asked.

'Mister, I don't know,' Harrington answered. 'But I know there's one thing you ain't going to do.'

Pigs may have small mean eyes. But I rather think I prefer life in a pig barn to life out here in the big wide world.